STURGE TOWN

POEMS

ALSO BY KWAME DAWES

POETRY
Progeny of Air
Resisting the Anomie
Prophets
Requiem
Jacko Jacobus
Shook Foil
Mapmaker
Midland
Bruised Totems
I Saw Your Face
Wisteria: Twilight Songs from the Swamp Country
Brimming
Impossible Flying
Gomer's Song
Hope's Hospice
Back of Mount Peace
Wheels
Duppy Conqueror
City of Bones: A Testament
Nebraska

With John Kinsella
Speak from Here to There
A New Beginning
Tangling with the Epic
In the Name of Our Families
unHistory

FICTION
A Place to Hide
She's Gone
Bivouac

NONFICTION
Natural Mysticism: Towards a New Reggae Aesthetic
Talk Yuh Talk: Interviews with Anglophone Caribbean Poets
Bob Marley: Lyrical Genius
A Far Cry from Plymouth Rock: A Personal Narrative

STURGE TOWN

POEMS

KWAME DAWES

PEEPAL TREE

First published in Great Britain in 2023
Peepal Tree Press Ltd
17 King's Avenue
Leeds LS6 1QS
UK

ISBN 13: 9781845235741

Supported using public funding by
ARTS COUNCIL
ENGLAND

We are the darkness, as we are, too, the light…
—— Barry Lopez, *Horizon*

For
Kojo, Adjoa, Gwyneth, Kojovi

For Mama the Great

For
Sena, Kekeli and Akua
and for Lorna for being there always

Remembering Aba, Neville

CONTENTS

I

...the rapid softening of light...

II

...all of light's fruitfulness...

III
...slowly, from shadow to light...

IV

...I close my eyes to push/ away the darting lights...

V

...Build me a house of light...

I

...the rapid softening of light...

BEFORE THE RETURN

Seeded by "scenes of a village" from my father's
In Sepia, chronicle of his making as a boy –
this before Walcott's *In a Green Night* –
every imagining of a return is a myth.
In the forensics of art, it is not hard
to trace the borrowed things,
the stolen things: my father's village, thick
with the scent of rum, where the ghosts
of slaves inhabit the heavy-leaved
guinep trees.
         Every thought of return
to the ancestral ground begins at night,
in an airport hotel, waiting for the next flight –
the lines of a city. Tomorrow, the green,
the incessant green, the worn-down building,
the broken tombs, the legend of my making.

TRAVELLING

For my grandmother

Sister Amelia Clarke gathers her books,
her black-rimmed spectacles,
and drifts further into the rocks
far from the salt and stench
of the beach head.

She cuts through the red water
like a boat at dawn
knifing the breakers,
contemplating the end of the horizon
where land nudges the waves
for a place in the sun.

She has seen the single file
of shackled children, eyes lost in mystery,
waiting to feed the bottomless pit
of those vessels swaying on the waves,
manacles new and glowing with sweat.

She has seen worlds beyond that line of the sea –
the journeys taken to the white cliffs of Dover,
the Tower of London, the Babylonian gardens, the Taj Mahal,
the sphinx, the pyramid caught in sandstorms,
the soaring buildings of New York.

From this rocky promontory
Sister Amelia Clarke has journeyed
and returned
to find her home still intact,
the compound still dusty,
the children still screaming,
the dogs still howling
through the night.

REBURIAL

There on the black sand they line up,
feet curled around dried fish bones,
their robes whiter than the surf
ticking on the slick green rocks.

They sing of Nyankopon, the giver of small mercies,
whose name was known but not understood,
who will insinuate his new name into the holiness
carrying them home, as if shouldering the world
on his broad back, broad head, broad smile.

And the preacher-man stands tall against the pull
and push of the Atlantic, this graveyard of many —
the fishermen swallowed by her soft mouth,
the leaping warriors defying the slaver's whip,
the diseased corpses unceremoniously tossed —
this Atlantic garden of bones curled around his legs.

And the believers in single file
enter the warm wash of salt,
the sky pink as coming blood.

Here on this crisp morning,
Reverend Clarke dips his daughter into salvation,
dips her far back, dips her low, so low that water
noses to her eyes bringing tears,
so low the cleansing salt stains her brain,
so low the mouth swallows death,
till rising in an arc of sudden light and water
she shouts in sync with the handclaps
and stomp of the believers.

Cough, they say.
Cough the devil from your heart.

Cough the clutter of death from your heart.
Cough the old breath out.
The new water has come, they say,
the new water has come.

THE PRODIGAL CONVERSES WITH THE LAND

1

Cape Coast:

I am a city in translation. What I say to you is not in the language
I carry. You will never understand the pidgin of my soil

because you are always a foreigner. It is true
that your grandmother's bones are interred in me,

and I know you hoped that by returning to me
you would hear her speaking. But you must know

that even more desperate people have come,
asking for some sound to carry through.

At least you know that I was named by white people,
and they have left the noise of atrocities here,

so that when those who come back, year after year,
instead of speaking of the drama of the ocean

beating against the shore, instead of the shouts and songs
of the fishermen dragging their catch across the dark sand

for the women to collect and take to the market, instead
of the clubs, the hi-life, the scent of bread baking at night,

instead of the deep forests that reach the edge
of the sea, and the way the sunset falls over Elmina,

instead of this, all they can talk of are the ones
who were collected here and taken across the waters,

only to return as interlopers, people with foreign tongues,
who do not understand our language of centuries.

We are the Akan. We are warriors, the broken companies
of the Oguaa. This means nothing to you. What you know

is the smell of soap and algae in the gutters, and the way the brine
in the lagoons thickens in the air; the addiction to *akara*

and the tart heat of pepper; and the tom-ba, tom-ba
of the mortar and pestle, the familiar sounds of heart and hearth:

these are the things that you will talk about, places
of nostalgia, of home. But all places know themselves

by the blood that has been shed there, the sadness
that will always haunt the laughter of this place.

Here is that church where your Mammy, the Pentecostal woman,
found her own Jesus, saw the coil of a python on the heavy shoulder

of her daughter, your mother, and they cast out the demon curse
on her, freed her from what would have consumed her.

She was young then, the age of your youngest
daughter. But she remembers, Chochoo remembers.

2
Kwame:

I know that the invention of memory, the silence before memory is made –
the imagined comfort of language, though failing every time,

though betraying my inner head and liver – is what I have,
is what we all carry. I lied when I said I found

the translation of this land into something like a nation,
or home, or comfort, or the spirits of ancestors –

I lied, and still I will say to you who stand at the gates
of this village, "Tell Mammy her grandson,

the one she teased, tell her he is asking to be let in,
and he is craving her fresh baked bread."

BEFORE THE MEMORY

Mammy is leaving.
We are gathered on the top of the stairs watching.
Our mother is a child again,
trying to prolong the parting,
and Neville sits silent
in the corner, fiddling
with the tape recorder.

Mammy sings.

Her farewell is a song about Nyame,
a plaintive dirge-like song in a minor key,
and we, in this pink morning,
know that this
will be a memory to cherish.

Our mother weeps,
falling on her mother's breasts,
and the tape recorder ticks in the corner,
while, there on the stairs,
we feel the pain in our chests.

Mammy gathers her sweep of cloth,
her basket and her bible,
and floats through the door.

AFTER THE DELUGE

Before the storms, the ground was red,
covered by the soil blown from foot-worn
football fields denuded of all grass.
Red, too, were the pavements in front
of the old shops, the abandoned
offices, the empty schools, the hollow
echoing corridors of the Old City Hall.
Before the storms, before the invasion
of the righteous militias, before
the executions against the limestone walls
in the alleyways, the city breathed
its own sweet liveliness,
and even the desperate knew how
to sing. Everyone could read the skies,
knew to look between the two
mountain peaks to find the making
of storms – even a child could time
the deluge to the second, its applause
shimmering across the zinc roofs.
But on the morning of the great storm,
the mountains vanished and blackness
swallowed the circle of hills.
The rain consumed the people
and left them with empty streets, mud-stained
walls, and roads black with flooding.
There are no ghosts here. They drained away
with the ebbing waters. What is left
is the soft wind off the river and the hum
that comes with the loss of all memory.

WELSH

For Neville

You smoked a pipe,
loved to stare in the camera's eye,
made of it a twinkle or a wink.
Those were the days of gin and tonic,
the days when you believed in the magic
of your fertile brain, when they hailed
genius in your body, the mastery
over bat and ball, the lithe
youthful walk, the muscles
alert, full of suicidal daring.
That was you. So perhaps
it was no surprise when
in 1949, in a small pub
in Wales, where the regulars
were so coal-stained they called
themselves niggers, they
thought a man who could play
the piano like you, drink like you,
run a hundred yards like you,
and fill your pipe with aroma
like you, had to be at least
as good as the worst Welshman,
and that was good enough
for the twisting, twirling Shakespearean
rag, fa-la-la, fa-la-lee, la-la.

NIGHT MUSIC

We who lived with the streets at our ear,
the flimsy zinc to guard us from predators,
who gathered in kerosene light to hear
the sweating politician promise us bread
and the dignity of a manifesto made of our blood;
we who, waiting for dawn, knew the yeast
smell of dough warming to swell
overnight in the heat, the wood-smoke rising
in the mud oven where embers glowed;
who knew the lamentation of the wind
in trees, or the giddy industry
of a bicycle's wheels ticking through the night;
who bathed in the algae-covered slick
of concrete, water flowing in a jet
over our bodies; who covered our bodies
in talc, our foreheads with Limacol,
the backs of our necks with rose-water;
who left our Sunday garments
to wave like flags in the wind; who
slept to the soft quarrelling of Carlos
the postman – "Jesus, I'm drunk, drunk,
drunk, my body can't work, oh no…";
who knew there was music in the soft hope
of these streets of standing pools of water;
who prayed as if there *was* mercy in the hills
from whence cometh our help; we dreamed
of bodies softly opening to us as a song
of the sea, in a room anointed with the green
incense of smouldering mosquito coils.

GATED

Raised in a city of clanking gates,
the tinkling of metal symphonies
of welcome, the ritual minutes looking
through the ornate grill while keys clang,
searching, testing their assortment
in the locks, with the final long music
of chains unleashed, the squeaking
hinge, the sound of desire
unhinged, our anticipation was another
marvel of welcome or fear – "Come
in, come in." In this city of wrought
iron, of rusty metal cages –
what kept them out is what
kept us in – the road was viewed
in fragments through tiny windows,
and our hearts, held steady in the language
of metal on metal, the un-coding
of distance and proximity, waited
always for love or dread in the shadows.

POST TRAUMATIC

Of course, I wonder about the sweet
avuncular poet who throws small
clues like "I have been sober
for a decade", and you ponder
what he was like then. He knows
cramped and seedy compacts in Delhi,
Managua, Joburg, and the way
a jungle smells in South Africa;
and you hear this music in his poems,
the sorry song of pure beauty.
But it is the pauses that halt you;
the way, out of words,
he does not look away, but keeps
fixed on your eyes as if waiting for you
to blink, but you can't. You are caught,
and so you say thanks, and he smiles,
asking you for what, before he says,
"Do you know Allman Town?" And you
know he means Kingston in the 1970s
and he doesn't smile about that, just asks,
like he is a tourist remembering.
Then he shakes your hand and the weight
of his thumb makes you wince,
before he limps away, his body
taller than you expected.
Late at night, you remember
a line you know will haunt
you for days with its symmetry:
"A good fortuner can always find a job."

THE LAST DUPPIES

I no longer trust the accidental art
of the wind, the random detritus
strewn in the barren yard of a community
caught in the limbo of decay and development.
The villagers, with the aid of astringent herbicides
and mortgages, no longer expect to see them.
At night, streetlamps and the sound system
for the dance session, jerk pork pans,
red stripe, rum and the flat screens
flashing their otherworldly colours consume
the comfort of darkness. In the early
morning, the rusting chain-link fence
yields a new installation of garbage.
These days, I imagine the last duppies
creating a shibboleth of defiance,
their last fantastic hauntings, along with
the last healers, the last herbalists,
marking their place in the last of the village.

RECALL

Reggae's insinuating bass cleaves to my bloodline.
All is quiet under southern skies.
Tomorrow I will go blind for what I have not seen.

It's a price I must pay.
Tomorrow, my last laugh will scatter over the dry leaves
of live oaks' shedding. I have heard no ragamuffin

in months. I have forgotten the roll
of my waistline, the offbeat skank.
It is like grief, this emptying, this silence,

waiting for the rush of stones.
I am dreaming now in a smooth southern drawl,
and we have found the muddied bodies,

eye sockets and teeth dragged from the swamp
by FBI agents in their clean white shirts and walkie-talkies.
The reeds are unmoved; they swing back in place

like rubber. Been watching too much
Mississippi Burning and *Eyes on the Prize*.
Still, it's true that they lynched someone in Florence

a month ago. On the roadside, a rusting Cadillac,
once green, now chewing grass sloppily
from its gaping windows and bullet-riddled skin,

ticks in the heat. I am dreaming in blue notes,
gospel calling, responding, sing-talking,
yes, swing-talking my way to salvation.

Oh, pipe me back to my familiar earth,
for it is slipping slowly from me.

WANDERER

How quickly the long-breathed dusks
of summer are wheezing, the light's
softening rapid here in the August end.
The scent of winter, months away,
is already filling the air, and this alien knows
that he's growing familiar with Nebraska.
And yet I don't understand the language
of these long pieces of stripped wood
laid out as a trellis might be, three strips
tied together with the thin bark of local trees,
and then propped up as fragile monuments
of hope or petition, some message
which I do not understand.
But despite my ignorance, I feel a desire
to fall to my knees and make my appeals,
as if such love is given upon request.
How does one say, "Please love me",
so as to be loved fully without question,
despite being unworthy, despite not knowing?
But, I hesitate, stay standing sinfully,
and say, "I am not against your faith,
yet, I continue mine" – which is the immigrant's
protest, as old as strangers arriving in a village,
as old as new believers praying in ancient temples.

PORTFOLIO LATINAMERICANO

El camino, *el burlador*, the guttural speakers
in cold stone homes; the flare of woollen
fabrics dyed with the colours that frighten
spirits and seduce the dead; the roasting of meat;
the clouds tumbling riotously off mountains
down into the dank mute walls and wet cobbles
of the city; the rum, the cuatro, the drum;
the woman standing naked near the last tree
before the river, her nipples brown as stones
at the water's edge; the way the ferns
and the drying mud along her shins
suggest the dream a grown man has
while he sips thick black coffee
in a decaying city; the brick walls
pocked with bullet holes – the old news –
paper photos on those same walls lined
with men in baggy dishevelled clothes,
with eyes mutely resigned to martyrdom;
the soldiers smoking before the execution.
I dream the road to Cartagena where all clichés
arrive: a gathering of itinerants,
their shirt-backs wet with sweat, eating
roasted fish and cassava, and days' old bread,
waiting for the truck to take them
to a future that must always return
them to what they have left behind.
Beyond them the sky is endless,
and here they are, aligned as uncertain
notes on staves, reaching for a music
that will consume the man in his cups.

THE MAN IN THE BLUE COAT

for Toussaint of Bréda

These dreams of the ancestors of my dignity
are distractions against the noise

of the elegies gathered in the lavender-soaked
silk kerchiefs of verse – the smoke and decay

of the almost dead kept in. I line up these neatly
rolled-up metaphors of what we keep

inside, keep hidden – the hope of a better time.
The light here in Nebraska is tender

and I walk the silent streets when the second
sunset arrives and the world is golden

with the softening of edges. From the top of the hill,
I see the slow stride of the man in a blue coat

with epaulets of gold. He has the bearing of a soldier,
walking across the avenue of leaving elms,

the way a general walks across the parade ground.
I call to him, but he is too far away to hear.

When I arrive at the fork in the road, he has disappeared;
the light has softened now to the mute

shadow of dusk. I return to the house, my body
already cool from the sudden drop in the temperature.

GARDENIA LEAF ON A WHITE WALL

after Anthony Hernandez

Archeologists, I am told, imagine
the earth as layered sheets, their texture
and density a kind of divination
of an empire's fate: what will be left
standing, what will eventually fall.
When I imagine what lies below
this land of mastodon bones, old enough
to seem like inventions, solid enough
to worry the faith of begats upon begats,
I think of this wall mapping our future.
The last layer before sky is us, and then
the deeper lines until we find ice and icing.
History is easier when seen close up,
the detail in the moment.
Stare long enough, all tangential
narratives become annoying blurs,
feathery inconveniences.
This is why we say that the leaf,
dark green and ill-shaped at the corner
of the wall, is the leaf of the gardenia,
whose scent, defying the cleansing of ice,
is the scent of freshly picked joy.

STURGE TOWN

i

In this fantasy of home-
coming, the termites,
out of respect, have vacated
the elegant homestead of delicate
filigreed panels and jalousies
that speak of a century ago,
and allowed the trees
to crowd in and shelter
the graveyard, the pimento
barbecue and the porch,
until the return. Of course,
the house is rotting;
the squatters abandoned
it for better walls,
and the prodigals
have not returned.

ii

For too long I spoke of return, a kind
of prodigal fantasy, although, face
set against the sun, I had abandoned
the waywardness of the failed son.
My father is long dead, and I was
faithful to the last. Still, postcolonial
that I am, I built my own myth
of departure, set aside the romance
of the exile for the pragmatics
of family and mission. Return
was to what might have been
had my ancestors lived longer,

had they held on to the cottage
on the hill. To Sturge Town's
pimento barbecue decks,
the green of an island's history
marching along the narrow paths
of the enslaved trodding
to the cane fields, I return as one
who visited once. Still, my heart
goldens in warmth to see
the grey slab with DAWES
etched into stone.

II

...all of light's fruitfulness...

IT BRUISES, TOO

Find words to describe the stone
heavy in the bowels, the disasters
we make of our lives, the haunting
that has killed before. You find me,
a clumsy journeyman, on a road
that curls across green plains.
You'll see me with my staff
from many miles away. I follow
the contours the mountains make
of the road until, hours later,
after two light showers
and a burst of sunlight, we meet.
I tell you I am doing penance,
and swear that the words
I am speaking are the breaking
of a long fast, that my voice
sounds alien even to me.
You ask why I wince like that.
"The silence," I say. "It bruises, too."
Then, after the elation of this meeting,
we part, you towards the light, me
into the gloom you left behind.

A YEAR

Taken from afar, every year is historical,
even if not while inside it;
so, 1962 was a year of great moment:
my father had a second son, had a book
doing the rounds of reviews,
was as much a writer as he would
ever be. It was his best moment
despite the doldrums he felt trapped in,
despite his impatience for glory
(he would not know this for years).
That summer he drank more to be giddy,
to be happy, to be so alive in the world –
the year my mother was his pride.
He rubbed her feet and rarely
shouted before breaking into tears –
the ritual she had come to know
in this alien lover of hers with his
native desires and obroni affectations.
Their friends gathered and thought him
a demigod for the gift he'd worked
so hard to make, that book, that last
enchantment; and then the other gift,
the one from God – though he was careful
to credit the muscularity of his hips –
me, the one he did nothing for. I just
came along, wet, pale and hungry
for air. It was a good year;
I say it was, so that is how it is.

REHEARSAL FOR LOVEMAKING

After the familiar clasp of a mother's
hand – the cupping and coaxing,
the rough caress, the search
for dead skin and itinerant dirt,
the fingers slick with ointment
probing into the orifices of sacred
privacy with casual, tender ownership –
a body will readily learn to accept
the proprietorial hands of a lover.
For quietly, as with all true
lessons, the body has recorded,
in small details, the dialect of love.
A boy sitting on a stool, fixated
by the cascade of clumps
of hair onto the elegant folds
of a white cloth, has never imagined
his hair to be so light, so delicate,
is easily distracted from
all the hair discarded, so much so
that he barely notices the firm hand
on his neck, its intimate coaxing
and guidance, the palm on the scalp,
the hooked finger under the chin,
the brush and press of a clumsy stomach,
the shared rhythm of their breathing,
his trust in the machinations of those hands.
In time, he will learn that there,
in this silent ritual of barbering,
the staunching of blood wounds,
the ministering of herbs and oils
from the open palm, the cup that runs
over, is a kind of love, the rehearsal
of the dance all true lovers know.

WHAT A FATHER GIVES

There was an impatience in your genius
that was admirable if never endearing,
the way you regarded as ordinary,
as the most common of gifts – competence,
as if it's there in the air, inviting anyone to pluck it,
and only a fool or a scatterbrain lets it slip by.
So, you instructed with callous disbelief
when you encountered someone who simply
could not do the ordinary, most humble of things:
hammer a nail straight, imagine the calculus
of wood, its substance, its bend, its swell,
the mechanics of shaving, cutting,
the pure exquisite grace of the snug fit
of plank with plank. Just use your head!
Look, look, look – easy as that! Were you
simply ignorant of your genius, the gift
you had been given? That would be quaint,
loveable, but you were so convinced
of the ordinariness of your craft
you imagined all of us should manage
to replicate it, that we were lazy, snobbish,
blind, not to be able to do the same.
I long envied and feared your elegant carpentry –
the gift so freighted with dismissive self-deprecation,
a gift you gave your daughter, so it became
hard to reassure her that she was not the product
of child labour, or one forced into the family trade,
but that her hands and eyes, her brain of quick solutions,
her capacity to unlock the complex language
of flowers, trees, wood, stone, flour, and the secret
ingredients in food – that these were all
signs of grace, gifts of genius. But it helps to know
where it all comes from, it helps to know.

FATHERLESS

After a year, he was ashes. My store
of sorrow overflowed. Still, there was time to find

love, its language of desperation, me floored
by the fear of losing Lorna, all this wind

and whirl of desire. Nothing in me would sleep,
nothing in me would rest – call me hooked

to love or the need. I did not place flowers
on his grave, for there was no grave. I keep

his departure as a marker, and Lorna as my brook
of sustenance, what she has always been. See? Look!

THE CHILD LEARNS OF DEATH

Growing up in the home of the butcher,
the child soon learns the equations of death:
that a dead body has its uses; that skinned
with care, the goat's pelt, if rescued
from the spill of blood by a skilled butcher,
will dry with elegance and strength,
and the drummers from the shrine
at the other side of the mountain
will arrive, eyes red with revelations,
with burlap sacks of aromatic weeds
that smell as green as the goat
smells red. The butcher woman,
with her sinewy forearms and welcoming
grin, will point the men to the cord
stretched from mango to ackee tree.
The conclave of drummers will corner
in whispers, running their open palms
over the pattern of hairs before they select.
They can smell the sweet pepper
in the large pot of chopped-up
goat meat and bones and curry
with an infusion of raw coconut oil.
They do not remove their turbans
of pristine white as they fill plates,
squat and spoon fresh rice and goat
into their mouths. They say *ase*,
selah and slowly climb the hill.
The child learns the commerce of killing,
the economy of trade and the grace of art.

NEW REVENANT

Travelling again, I am running into
my revenant, the body remaking itself
in new landscapes — well, perhaps, not new,
but different. For two years my body
had grown used to its stable order,
its shape and presence until,
in the disquiets of travel,
I relearn its contours.

We land on the last stretch of land
before the Cape of Good Hope
where I await the scrutiny of my papers
with disquiet, my senses still tender
as an old wound to hear the clipped
syntax and phonemes of Afrikaners
speaking English — whatever music's there
tainted by 1980's memory, the films,
the lectures; this reinforced
by the stern official at the airport,
and later the twitchy maitre d'
questioning our presence at a buffet.

It's been an uncomfortable journey,
my body still holding in the news
of fit, grinning Biyi's sudden passing,
and my fingers still longing for the tender
memory of my aunt Povi's slender hands,
the sensation of last touches, the feel
of affection, skin on skin, and the scent
of gardenias on her elegant face,
when she welcomed me in the hotel lobby:
"Oh, Kwame, oh Jesus, and Kwame,
there is always one — our prophet,"
and me thinking, "Say 'poet',"

though I am tempted by the hubris of prophecy –
the desire to see further, and then speak.
How beatific her smile, how age humbles us, though
it was hard to tell if she was admonishing me
for my failure to fulfil all promises.

In the jungle of my words, I have begun
to admit the constant sorrow for what
is left of desire, the hunger always for light,
consuming light. My latest secret is the narrative
of being told how to face my last days –
the problem for aging poets that all
our metaphors are crowded out
by the plots we devise for our deaths.

So, I make two vows today, as we circle
Johannesburg: never economy, not any more,
for my name is Oga, Nana Kwame, and I must
fly with the comforts of an elder – this,
and the more difficult vow: to make poems
of beautiful things fiercely in their height
of oblivious delight – the persistent things.

KERATOCONUS

I cherish now all of light's fruitfulness,
this day of wars and quakes under the mute sun;
I repeat my songs of gratitude for being blessed,
and it seems like ingratitude for me to run
to that dark year I looked up to the trees
and saw what looked like streaks blurring the core
of the earth. That year, the doctors said shells
covered my cornea. They asked me to say more
about family history – the blindness, the bees
eating away at our light. All sight ceased that year.
I became a poet who sees through dying cells.

IT BEGINS WITH SILENCE

For Sena and Akua

The womb of the woman is the universe. The dark space
where all things begin and get completed…
From Dana Rothberg's *White Lies* (2013)

My daughters, I will save you the trouble
of finding words for that meeting in the darkness,
of my eyes not discerning you, my gentle request
that you take my hands to your faces, to trace a memory
of love – the smile, the giggle in the shape of your lips.
My daughters, perhaps this will be the register of the dark
and light of last meetings, those repeated again and again,
and you will, I hope, walk into a long dusk, the light
perfect in its tenderness, your ordinary mundane
conversations about money, vacations, work,
your brother, your mother's anticipated questions.
This poem, I hope, will save you the scent
of my body decaying, the things I will keep about me,
the forgiveness, perhaps, of what you will know and not know
before you separate, drive towards your own futures.
On my walks, I am carrying you in my head, the mantra
of wished for things, the prayer for your laughter to never end
but to grow and grow in the soft depth of contentment,
the tenderness of your delight in open skies, the way
you return to the womb of belonging; that you will know
the persistence of being loved, the art of family –
remembering the dates, the anniversaries, the absurd
details, the lies we treat as games – knowing that lies
of deepest wounding are healed in the shadow of wombs,
the unreachable places that make the beginning and end.
It begins with silence, it begins with water, it begins with shadow.

FISH, SERPENT, EGG, SCORPION
For Kekeli

> *For everyone who asks receives; he who seeks*
> *finds; and to him who knocks, the door will*
> *be opened. What father among you, if his son*
> *asks for a fish, will give him a snake instead?*
> *Or if he asks for an egg, will give him a scorpion?*
> — Luke 10-12

There were no tears, but in the commotion
of these emotional days, the impetus for tears,
when I said to him, there in the cold street,
wearing our sporty winter jackets, "I am your gift,
this body before you, still here to say, *Let's take a walk, son,*
me, this complex of secure love. I am not
your enemy, not a murky pond of dangers. Don't you
know that when I was your age, my hunger
for a shelter in a man's heart was already dust?
He was dead, gone, and all I had
was the surrogates of his letters, the clues
of a narrative of love in his fiction and poems,
the snippets of affection from his old friends –
hardly enough – but all I had upon which to build
an edifice of meaning. And I wrote then,
World, world, world, that I have lost – full of every
melodrama of mourning, though it was never
hyperbole, never a lie. I said to him, "So here I am."
And my voice was phlegmy and earnest,
"Here I am for you, so use me, feed on me,
I am your father, use me." Perhaps we must all
say this, or have thought to say this, we who father
sons. Maybe. Every poem has its own ancestry,
but this was us, me embracing him, and him saying,
"Sorry, Dad, I know." And even now, it breaks me
that I could present him with my body,

my mortality, my leaving him; that I could let
him feel the start of his long mourning before it
has to come. I said, "I could die today", not as hyperbole,
but as a truth that runs through my veins, my lungs.
This is love, then, a father and a son, him handsome,
fluid, tender, the boy and man, all there, and me
mourning for his bereavement. It was a passing thing.
We re-entered the house with the noises of the season,
laughter, even as if that moment between us
could be set aside. Of course, we know it will not be.
I know that this father must say again and again,
"I am made for you, and I will not promise you a fish
and then hand you the threat of a serpent."

NOT JOY'S PROPHET

I weigh words of caution – clipped wings,
warnings of dangers to come – though all
ahead seems clear, flash points, red flags,
how springs turn so easily into floods of disaster,
how, fever-fit, we can grow dark with regrets.
I know I am not joy's prophet, just a father
recounting moons passed, nervous that every word
I say will annoy them, indolent to my warnings.
It is a painfully cold day, and the high noon
is relentless; all I cry for is common-sense!

It's thirty years since my crossroads, my core
changed by migration. In those days, dreams
were built on nothing but promise: "Go o'er"
was then the blood of my art. The sun beamed
on us, bowed in conference. Maybe I fell
into the simple art of survival. It was grey
in Sumter before I knew the name for the vines
stretched green across bridges. Today my children,
their lot once mine – with rent, bills, infants,
new wife – have said farewell to youth.

AGAINST THE ELEGY

Damirifa due
Damirifa due

We have come through the soft silence of the night, the nurses'
bodies retreating with the sway of women who have learned to preserve
themselves for the sudden alarm. They move through dim halls
with their soft-spoken complaints, judging each shift by the troublesome
ways of the sick. I long to ask if there is a proper way, how to make hands tender,
but I dare not ask. They appear and disappear. When, Aba, you say tablet,
she hears you saying, "I want to stab you!" And forgive me for wishing her right.
This is what "day-to-day" means, the tiniest battles, the triumph
of bowels moving, and the extra spoon of insipid porridge, the sudden light
of morning – the way the mountains rise above the peeling paint
of the loading deck. There is a view of God's grace above the daily
betrayals. The prayer asks if it is the holiness of the prayed-for
that turns the head of God, but who knows the calculus of miracles?
I have asked because you said I should; I ask as a bargainer,
Abraham haggling for mercy, convinced as all keen hagglers are
that no market-God will present the true price first. The ritual of trust
is the ritual of deal-making. I am carrying in my head the gathering
of rain clouds, a melody that will not let me go. I hum it,
hoping you are receptive to its familiar scent: the chapel
in the hills, bodies young enough for hope, poinsettias riotous
as hallelujahs, and the voices arriving like the whisper of rain over land.

ELEGIAC

For Kojo

Eventually, what remains is all head, the sculpted
dignity of a face, beautiful in its authority —
the lips, the smoothly embossed eyelids, the jutting
noble forehead. Your body is the case that holds
the arteries that circulate the weekly cleansed blood,
the machine pumping, rituals of fatigue and more fatigue,
and then some relief on the third day — a space to let
the muscles rest. I am startled by the relief of what
I will become, dear brother, what we must all become,
the body waning to bone and tautness.
My embrace expected the gathering of sullied flesh
but what I feel are your fragile bones.
You are wearing dark expensive shades —
you've always liked the finer things — call it
stylish blindness, and your beard's a mercy of texture
and grace — how neatly she has trimmed it for you,
carving out your beauty, white against mahogany.
All that remains is the beautiful head, the animated
dignitary defying posterity in the heroes' gallery,
the pedestals of busts lining the walls like the spoils
of barbaric wars, though your face is not macabre
but endearing as an old comfortable revenant,
returning me to the nobler shadow of my too, too, solid self.
There is no language for this mourning before the news.
Still, we who are cursed with the good fortune of years
have learned to rehearse the heavy sorrow of our loss.

THE FORGETTABLE LIFE

I do wonder how it is inside him that he can live
unknown or unknowable. Not so much the details
of his life: birth, education, travels, the journey
to London to make a life, arriving on a ship in worn
shoes; the return to Kingston, the job, the school,
the factory, the loss of the factory, the house built,
the islands visited, the places with small, clean, humble
rooms smelling of floor polish and boiled cabbage
where he tucked away his quiet self, his body
barely occupying space. No, it was not these,
the observable details, nor the six children,
some almost alien to him now, others intimate
with managed love – the rituals of stoic affection,
tempered by silent resentment, the mix of anger
and gratitude: the things unsaid, the lugging of all this
from stage to stage of unsettled lives.
No, not even this, but the things that are hidden –
the moments of regret, of desire, the way
in Kingston he saw another morning growing
over the mountainside from his back window;
the efficiency of his grief the morning
he buried his wife – and all the space she left.
The children, thankful for his steady persistence,
still wonder whether it is love that makes men
soon follow their wives, and what it was that
made him not follow her – his quick tears, his
tender nod, his pragmatic resolve to press on,
though he always thinks of her gently,
after all those years together, and she the survivor
of the sorrows of being orphaned.
I think of how we live our lives unseen
by those who should know,
and how, at death, the scent of things
fades with us into tidy compartments,

the manageable, compact world we try to hold
as a container of chaos, that even we
do not admit we keep. I ask him to tell
me about this, while he builds a shelf
with tidy efficiency, nothing left to chance.
He pauses over a nail, ponders for a minute,
then smiles and stares at the leafless trees.

IRIE ITES

From you the prayer for peace is not a borrowed song,
not the exotic skin worn by colonising, kleptomaniac poets

with the deepest alertness to the treasures to be discovered
among the lesser tribes; for you this prayer is the lament

of a man whose body has been invaded by sorrow and the grace
of his mother tongue. To plead against the catastrophes

of the marauding plague and the traders of decay and destruction
is a holy gift, a benediction for a dearly mourned mother,

her ashes now a memory in the air to her son.
I consider the vertigo of my days,

as if I am still mourning my sister's death, the deepest
absence that will not relent. When I said, "All is changed,

my self, known and loved, is gone," I was opening my heart's
hunger to the persistence of these wounds of loss.

I sway with the calm of one awaiting the news
of the end of things; it is now a matter of moments,

every sun-dazzled day a miraculous gift, the brawta
of a man's life: the extras, the unearned mercies, the gifts.

On Sunday, I ran across old Toussaint – which offends him,
this "old" business, since we have the same age,

though he does have a lean and hungry look. And though I say
I ran into him, I knew I would find him outside the grey walls

of the old catholic chapel. I knew he'd be there
long after mass while the last light spilled over the grass.

He, of course, opened the door for me, and asked me to sit.
He gave me half of a banana and smiled as I ate.

Then he knelt, and I saw his lips move without sound, the same
small word rising tenderly, illuminating the sanctuary.

DEATHWATCH

It is, of course, old Wallace Stevens,
austere as a cow in autumn,
polite, blandly circumspect,
curled lick of hair above the long black
coat, who stands watch, waiting for you,
and you again have the taut skin
of an infant, your body covered
in a thin sheet as if already wrapped
for burial, the neat lines
spindling out like ripples of a pond,
your eyes turned to that sweet
sister of yours, in her chair,
watching over you, helpless
as a saint who knows all too well
that the rest is not our affair.
Mr Stevens says nothing; he is
kindly but that is because
you know how careful he is
with the arrangements, the paperwork,
and when he says, with a ticking
dry tongue, "Well, it is all in order now,
you can have a good death", you know
he makes his poems as an accountant
calculates what is in hand
and rarely considers what is to come.
"Protect me," you say to your sister,
with her pointed nose and crooked
stick. She stares at Mr Stevens,
then mutters softly, "It will be fine,
sweetie, you go..." And you know
she has not heard you, you know,
for you have not spoken.

AT ANCHOR: THE REAL SITUATION
for Bob Marley,
Bavaria, October 1980

In the brilliant morning on a fishing boat,
a dying man dreams of Jamaica,
of the murmur of soft waves.
Here, at anchor, apart from the ordinary lull
of the easy tide, there is peace.
He cannot know that, in seven months,
the weight of wool on his shoulders will be lifted,
that in the soft gloom of a German chalet
in deep January he will anticipate with terror his death,
rewriting his theology of eternity, shadowed
by the swirling clouds, the bickering sycophants,
the friends who will not stop to pray,
frightened as they are by the end of the crusade.
Here, he already knows that his last songs
convey the weight of a man sitting by the sea,
staring out into its slithering metallic green
and imagining his words as prayers,
for a truth unfettered by the promise
of another morning. The sea is so unremarkable
that it becomes an exquisite maw. What a lofty
standard of beauty that is for a song.

INTIMATIONS OF GREATNESS

Rolling in from the verandah through the French
doors, chased into shelter by a sudden
squall misting the sea, he comes through the hall
of paintings made year after year with a sense
of failure – the condition of the above
average painter who has dreamed of greatness –
no, not just dreamed, but courted it, tested
himself against those he considered great.
When he was young and handsome,
they called him an asshole, an arrogant type,
and perhaps he was, for anyone could see
the pride he felt in the lack of kink
in his hair or the shame he felt at the way
the sun turned him into a cliché of himself.
His friends were legion, men walking
through ancient cities, the ruins of mountain castles,
all the makers of art, and people he never met
but lived with, quarrelled with, envied with
each stumbling line, living like this decade
after decade, waiting to be called one of the greats.
And now, here on his island, a man
with nowhere else to go, a man who cultivated
complete disdain for his followers, is waiting
for the dead to rise out of the sea, those
heavy-headed geniuses of a civilisation
that still scorn his tiny Patmos of an island,
to beckon him out in the garden
to walk among the *arboles*, to go home.

DEPARTURE

Repent, says the scratch-voiced rain man on the moon.
Repent, says the cricket on the moon,
dubbing on the moon, reggae on the moon.

The small boat with a lone body moves with soft intent
towards the blurring of light; you know that she,
this wizened woman whose arms are sinewy with labour,
understands that her aberrant soul writes its epics
on her body, in her body. At seventy, she knows
she still can conjure the transparent honey
of her vagina with a dream, with a thought
of the super-ape in the moon, her dub organising
old friend, the one who found her this shelter inside
the mountain. From the vantage point of the inland beach,
among the cicadas, where they made fires night after night,
and told each other stories of music, of history
and ancestry, until they found what they always
knew they would, their common ancestor,
the great, great grandmother, long enough past
for secrets, but not long enough for sin. Repent, repent,
she says to the nation. Repent your fallen ways!

And the man in the moon, her blood cousin,
her lover, her dream-stirrer, shakes his shoulders
with laughter and echoes back at her, Repent, repent!
And the cave booms with their laughter.

MOURNING SKY

We only know God is in the sky
by the sliver of two slight bodies
at the foot of the Blue Mountains.
Under epic clouds, a tumult of shadow
and light, see a woman and a girl
standing beside a tree. The woman
will remember the sky years later,
like lucky ones remember desire or miracles.
It is dawn. The woman says,
"It is time for you to wash your hands."
She leads the girl into the shadows
and there is to be no sent ram
to halt the blood and the wounding.
The girl will remember the sky
like the unlucky remember loss,
the things we have lost that have no name.

STUCCO

These walls are made of stucco
over brick, the thick lime milk
stirred with a leafy twig in a cheese pan,
then scooped in palmfuls –
you feel the chemical heat
of the mineral on the skin –
as clumps and clumps
are piled on, then smoothed,
the layered whiteness against the brick
creating another skin of our aging,
generations on generations,
repeated on the eve of some festival,
a wedding, a christening, or the visit
of a priest, a relative returned,
the council man, or the warner
woman who arrives, as a doctor might,
to sit, eat cake, sip tea, and listen,
before her pronouncement
changes the path of someone
in the house. Or, perhaps, it's
when a woman returns home
and sees the sun hit the side wall
in such a way that she thinks
it would give her pleasure to see
this wall cleansed of all the stains
of living, the line almost as black
as dried blood where the flood rose
and stopped before receding,
or where the dust storm stained
everything a patina of red,
like some wounding.

This is the house of Lee –
we call it the Ancient House of Lee –

the name invented for a Kingston
that existed before my arrival.
The family of Lee are gathered.
A child leans out, her face turned away,
the part-line of her braids running down
the centre of her head. In this moment,
we hold our breaths, arrested by her stillness,
as if we could smell her if we breathed,
as if she has spilled out of the window
and been there for days and days –
until she moves, until her shoulders
shudder. Then we know she is in tears,
and the world grows tense with the wondering,
this dark body against the gleam of lime.
This is when I think, that in this child
is the secret of our future, the secret
we carry inside us, the making of guilt,
of regret, the seeds of our formed selves,
the first layer of a future that will grow thick
with the warm protection of our rituals of forgetting.

IN THE WILDERNESS

The ragged horizon on the outskirts of town
is where I come to pray, on a stretch
of deserted land, abandoned
after a foreclosure, solitary electric poles,
lined up like the signs of an ancient war –
crucifixes for the traitors of promise,
the great folly of greed. The air is brittle,
an atmosphere clear of chemicals,
as if a century has passed since
the great explosion – as if I am
the one driven out into the wind.
My mouth grows dry. How odd
that I expect a voice in the silence
to tell me where to turn. I pass sixty
this year. I fear already how it will end –
this sugar in my blood. In this open field,
the revelation leaves me sombre.
The sun settles in on my skin;
everything grows dry as eternity.

AT THE CEMETERY

After Mario Algaze's *Portfolio Latinoamericano*

Eventually, Tio Eugenio, after the untidy chaos
of shovels leant carelessly on the tombs,
with the broken straw hat and the worn
jacket of the gravedigger's apprentice;
after the broken soil has refilled the grave,
soil scattered about to make room
for your unpolished casket that smells
too freshly of newly felled trees,
and the turpentine in the sealant;
and after all those shoes have departed,
tramping through the lanes, leaving
a cacophonous disturbance
of dust-robed earth, the bodies still sweating,
still fighting the rot at their core,
the cemetery warden will lock
the gates, searching the skies for rain.
In a few months, the bare earth
will be clothed in green grass,
and the vines we planted will run riot
over the stone and, on the corners
of the monument, the mould,
verdant and persistent, will remind us
that death is a silent companion
of the open sky. We will miss
you, *mi tio*, and then we will not.

BAPTISM OF DUST

We did all we should have done, bathed her,
held her sack of bones, gently, slipped on
the too-generous fabric of her before-life,
painted flesh and hints of life into her face
so that those who looked would not collapse
from sorrow, not so much for their loss
but from the terror of imagined suffering.
And as she wanted, we put him to the flames
as they had done to the house in the ghetto shelter
when he was taken to die in the hospital.
"Let it all be burnt away," he said to her,
"all these wounds in my skin, and may this dust
be purified by heat." We, a party of saints, apostates
and reluctant warriors, climbed the crooked path
to the cliff that looks over the Caribbean Sea,
our heads pointing to South America and the fantasy
of flight. This, too, he made us promise to do.
The gulls moved by with wise nonchalance,
as if death was ordinary as water. We stood
waiting to heal our stain, we who felt
contaminated by this death, this blood-and-water
wasting death. And who could have known
how the wind would turn or how far their son
would have to throw the ashes? But the wind
did turn, and the ashes, arrested in midair,
returned to us like spray off the sea, and we
were baptized in ash, our noses stuffed up,
our tongues dried with the taste of him,
our eyes stinging with his ashen self,
and what could we do, facing the farce
of it all, but tremble at our uncharitable fear,
trying to clear our throats discretely, our hearts
thumping from something like sorrow, like shame?

CONDOLENCE

Thrice this week, I send condolences to acquaintances
whose intimacy has grown the more by empathy – we are of an age
of sudden deaths, or the prolonged and painful passing of loved ones.
It is fall, and I know that we are all, in our small boxes,
dreading the dusk, knowing that trees turning orange and crimson,
will be, for years to come, the way we see our losses,
our complicated loves. So, when I write my condolences,
I scour the poets I trust – I know, at once, the inadequacy
of my own poems – how clotted they are with the details
of pedestrian news, with private names and anxieties.
I find Grimay's "Elegy" and note she has not said who is dead,
has described a lone hawk as an image of how we move
through the world longing for what we have lost.
I think how generous is the open-endedness of her sorrow,
how fitting to send to my three acquaintances,
so they will find themselves in the fall sunset reading
into their grief a kind of beauty. Yet I regret even this gift,
in the way, of late, I have regretted my body, the cupcakes
I devoured, their sour residue on my tongue, my blood
betrayed, my waning lusts; regret the sprawling words
written in journals years ago, that list things in the moment,
without a hint of how they record time passing. What remains
is gratitude to Grimay and her "Elegy", and the gift she offers me,
wordless in the face of what I know is to come, has come,
and will continue to come: nighttime, and the long, long sleep.

ELEGY FOR THE CANDLE MAKER

For Glendon

i

You dreamed of lighting all the dark
corners of the city with candles
scented with lavender, places where
the poor settle in shadows, thankful for
the occasional illumination of a car's
headlights casually swooping
over the walls before the second
and third darkness. You dreamed
of giving respite from the gloom to those
waiting for the sun. This is what
your hands could do, you said,
with the short, sharp glare of a smile.
You show your hands – the hands
of a man returned again from the dead.
This is what miracle hands can do,
what resurrection hands can do,
what Lazarus hands can do.

ii

You take the soft coil of white thread,
the wick, and lay it down on the wax-embossed
board. Then you stack the raw squares of beeswax –
the fuel, the persistence of life,
with their soapy scent, malleable as clay
when warmed – so that the light
from the broken window
spreads inside the wax, as if lit from within.
You take from the sill, where you
have lined vials of dye and silver saucers

with leaves and grasses of every aroma
you have imagined, crushing, rubbing
your fingers and sniffing, frowning,
searching for the scent of restoration
and replenishment. This, you say,
is what a man's hands can do
in the place between the emptying
of death and the reimagining of futures.
You know that the body can return
to walk the streets, marry into love,
dream of making babies laugh,
dream of filling the world with light.

iii

Glendon, may they, after the Sankey
and the tears, light a thousand candles
over your grave, and leave them there
to illuminate the last darkness we all
must enter, and may their light turn
the broken sepulchres and crypts into
a sudden temple of grace, here in the interim
between memory and forgetting.

AFTER "IT BRUISES, TOO"

i

Under a peace-loving drone's gaze,
purring its presence, above it all,

not seeking to startle, the drama enacts itself:
two bodies walk a mountain road towards

each other, appearing and disappearing
behind its slopes, bends and contours,

until, after the squall and the bright light
and deep shadow of moving clouds,

after an hour or so, they meet,
without fanfare, pause, and then

continue again. I know, as does
the controller thumbing the drone's throttle,

that were either of them to gaze upwards,
the sight of this object, eying them from above,

would terrify with the superiority of its farseeing eye –
the eye of the poet – and the disquiet of being

a small creature moving slowly through
the world, from shadow to light.

ii

This vision collapses into the Kingston memory
of a hawk's mothering scream,

diving towards my bare head,
the dizzying feeling tethering me to the earth.

We watch the destruction of bodies and streets
from the bloodless gaze of the drone's eye;

we make games of our terrors, nightmare
our ends in the inexorable zooming in of the eye

towards the target, towards the tower, towards the factory,
towards the church, all these continuing on a loop, again,

and numbingly again, until all terror is siphoned
from our world. I keep returning to the memory

of imagining a meeting from so far above, of
two people walking on their pilgrimages and meeting

at the point of accidental intersection, pausing,
exchanging pleasantries and prayers and blessings,

and then moving on, wondering if love,
perhaps repeated, could be the new healing.

III

...slowly, from shadow to light...

HUMAN RIGHTS

"if in the middle of my life
I am turning the final turn
into the shining dark
let me come to it whole
and holy
not afraid
not lonely."
— Lucille Clifton

After the vow, the incision and the ritual letting of blood, the priestess
begins her labours. She travels across Europe, not the tourist route,
       not the Riviera and boulevards,

but where the stash of the colonial enterprise, of imperialist endeavours
       is secreted – among those C.L.R. James
called the civilizations of moral turpitude, those that said:
       Find a people weakened by kindness,

overwhelm them with lies, with betrayals, plot murder by your operators,
practice deceit, live by deceit, master deceit, then slaughter, slaughter, slaughter.

To these capitals, with their columns of austere authority, where
       the prayers of others
have been stolen and brought to these catacombs of power, is where
       she goes.

She's made her charts of necromancy and holy larceny, and in
       each city, she stands before the spirits
of the living and the dead, held in a painful frieze in these bloodless
       tombs,and she draws,

as one sucking up all meaning from what she sees, collecting
       the stolen wisdom, the dark beauty
of steel and stone, of wood and rock. She sketches each piece with care,
       re-collecting,

she says, her stolen civilizations. She returns south, finally, to
       St. Vincent by boat, in a cotton dress
and dusty boots. She is carrying a satchel full of sketch books,
       rugged, leather-bound.

She waves down a taxi, and asks to be taken as far as the law allows;
       the windscreen
wiper pushes the soft dark ash of cataclysm, until, somewhere
       nondescript, the car slows.

"Yuh gwine ave to come off here," the driver says. Here the coconut trees
       have turned seaward
and the sky is dusk though it is still mid-morning. As soon as she
       steps out, her dress turns ashen,

her face covered in dust. From there she can see Soufriere's dark
       breath filling the sky –
there, as if to ritualize all beginnings, she watches this ancient cycle
       of destruction and birth.

She says to the dark air,
"*We have been known to put words into the mouths of spirits.*
God is too high, and justice too far away . . .
if it is western, if it is the final
Europe in my mind,
if in the middle of my life
I am turning the final turn
into the shining dark
let me come to it whole
and holy
not afraid
not lonely."

Ahh Lucille, amen, ase, ashes.

BONES IN THE SOIL

This landscape – the entanglement of trees,
the river valley, the music of light through mist,
the silence – seems empty, but I can't
sit still in the dark cave of this forest
and think of anything but troubled spirits, well,
not even that, but the bodies of black people
who died here, so ordinary, the limbs
so easily broken, the indignity of nakedness,
their squalid disposal the dead end of abuse,
their flesh becoming the offence
of a stench until the earth took them.

Today, a white man can walk his family's acres
with easel and canvas and brush and think: Silence,
the communion of trees, the confluence of rivers,
the chapel of light, the synod of forgetfulness.
I wish I could write myself into such distractions.

Perhaps that is what Zen offers; you clear
your head, let oxygen enter your bones, and soon
you will see the amber of fall as only that –
leaves turning. But me, I think bones,
I think bones restless in the dark soil.

THE VANISHING

I arrive in yet another clearing and sense
the kind of loss you feel when you arrive
the morning after the party, and even in
the cooling air the room stinks of stale meat,
sweet juices, sweat, the detritus of desire
like the lingering dew on the grass.
Of course, there was no party here,
not in this clearing deep in the forest,
not a party of bodies, although I can be forgiven,
standing among the petals of the crepe myrtles,
for imagining the dark naked bodies
of spinning dancers, while the soft pink petals
fall over them in the insistent glow of the moon.
Off to the east, once you locate the sounds –
the tick of insects, the call of blackbirds,
the revenants of their footfall – you can
hear the ocean's murmur, and there is the path
the dancers would have taken, following
the sea's pull, their bodies clothed in the sweat-
held petals. I envy them this vanishing.

THE MAKING OF A POET

Shadow me daily, says the poet to the clouds,
your dark cooling shall keep me safe;
the ficus shade shall soften my edges,
and the cool after the city's heat shall be
my cocoon, though the preacher says *Your sins,*
your sins, shall find you out.
I lived in government green-painted institutions
smelling of neglect and brute indelicate scrubbing
with wholesale industrial disinfectant,
with stale food and the funk of bodies
desperate to hold their dignity with talcum
and cheap creams – these the new day-girls
of Glenhope. I was there, a body untutored
in the grace of restraint, a boy, shy, hungry
to see the secrets of women emerging,
and at night, shadowing all secrets, I would
sit outside the TV room and watch
the rituals of desire at the compound's edge,
the girls furtively negotiating
the advances of the street boys.
Call me a voyeur, call me a kind of slut,
but I still carry the transgression of indulgent
watching, spying, in the shelter of night.

MENDACITY

In 1936, Walter Benjamin wrote
that the true storytellers were farmers
seeding the earth with myths of belonging,
and port-hopping, whoremongering
seafarers trading in tales from one dull land
to another, demanding a price for exoticism.
Ah, poor man, he did not know that the pathology
of storytelling is an intoxication with lies,
the helixes in our cells always imagining
beginnings and inventing futures that involve
our hunger to be loved, the myth
of our necessary presence. I stand here
with a mouthful of tales that I will share
like slivers of succulent fruit – until they turn
to dreams deep in the night. All beauty
will be marked by the first and last meals,
the fruit of knowledge and the bread
and assuaging wine of betrayal.
Sometimes, to survive, we forget this,
but it stays under our skins; it stains
everything. This is the envelope I mail
out each day; it is full of the sweet lies
of my deepest, most alarming truths,
those that stay inside our cells, in the way
that only contagions can stay, like farmers'
seeds of belonging, like the exotic
futures of old seafarers' tales.

VAGRANTS AND LOITERERS
South Carolina, c. 1950

You got that clean waistcoat, the bright
white of a well-tailored shirt,
you got those loose-as-sacks
slacks and some spit-polished shoes,
and you know, whether you are looking
like money, or about to take a stroll,
to tilt that hat like you own the world.
Yeah, smoke your pipe, roll your tobacco,
and, loose as authority, hold your muscles
lithe and hard, and every so often,
when you feel the urge, reach into
your waist pocket and pull out that watch
on its chain, look up to the sky and say,
Gonna be a cold one when it come,
like God gave you that fancy clock
to tell the future. These are the easy
boys of the good old South, waiting
for what is out of frame to happen:
the sheriff with his questions,
the paddy wagon, the chain gang,
the weight of the world.
Waiting, with such delicate dignity,
in a world as fickle as the seasonal sky.

ESHU OR AMBITION

Robert Johnson walked to the crossroads,
the place where the spirits chatter, and there
he met a large Black man. Some called him Satan,
some called him Legba, some called him Blues,
but, whoever he was, he took Robert Johnson's guitar,
and he played it well, and when Robert Johnson
returned to the land of the living, the small towns,
the juke joints, the bars, and the fields of elation
and suffering, he was transformed in ways
that let folks know he'd left something behind
with that big Black man. It bears saying,
for the sake of this poem, that Robert Johnson is me,
though my triumph was to leave the crossroads intact.
No one offered me the genius of hot fingers;
I waited, and the big Black man set the guitar down,
walked away with his bowlegs and strut, tossing back,
"Dat ting is out of tune." So, that was that.
Back in the square, no one turned their faces
from the glow of me, just a few polite nods,
and the dogs mooching along with their doggy
life, as the ancients liked to say; and me,
I returned to my hut and sat and watched the world
pass me by, my heart thick with love in search
of a home. Perhaps this is ambition, this persistent
hunger. Today is a day of stomach cramps,
the hollow melancholia of the interim, the slough
between mountains, and this is what it must be.

SORROW

In sooth, I know not why I am so sad,
It wearies me, you say it wearies you.
But how I caught it, found it, or came by it,
What stuff tis made of, whereof it is born
I am to learn.

—The Tempest: Act 1, Sc 1

It is low grade and unremarkable, my sorrow;
it comes like indigestion or shortness of breath
and the worries of these signs of weakness
no one need know. Of course, sorrow is
too much of a word, such a fat word, filled
with the bitter aftertaste of tepid coffee
left on a café table, the pink of a woman's lipstick
on the cup's rim, and a heavy chill over things.
It's the pretension of Mozart's *Requiem*
seeping under the door of the lonely man,
always lamenting what he has lost.
No, sorrow is the woman I met in Ganthier,
staring blankly into the cane fields, her feet dusty,
her skirt stained, her breath heavy with hunger.
She has nothing left; the litany of her losses
so epic, one cannot repeat them in a poem.
Mine is the insipid persistence of regret,
or perhaps the feeling that happiness is
the prelude to tragedy, or having an ankle
that sends sharp pains up my body
every few steps I take. I should have learned
to drink, but instead I have learned to chuckle
ironically, find quiet in the way things are.

WORK

Nine days to go, working for the next day
— Bob Marley "Work"

It is easy to slide over the word *work*;
take it to mean what it isn't.
Look at this man's hands, look
at the toughness in his fingers,
the way his nails darken at the edges,
the way his skin is marked
by old scars, the way his palms
are leather-tough – a grater of skin
if he drags them over your arm.
Those hands still remember
the grooves where the blisters
would settle and then harden
to toughness from holding the handle
of the clumsy seed-planter
bouncing on the uneven furrows,
planting, planting. Sometimes it's easier
not to know that on the plantation
out there on James Island,
every morning, seven days a week,
a bell sounds out, just thirty minutes
left before you line up by the fields
to start to sweat all day
to pay rent on that wood shingle
and mud chimney that they've given you.
And if you miss a day, your family
will lose shelter. That is work,
keeping the wolves from your door,
the left foot following the right,
the sickle swinging, the dirt
on your skin, and the shadow
over you when the script runs out.
Work is always behind, always owing

somebody something – payment in June
for debt from December when the cold
reached into your gut, held you down.
Work is one pair of shoes each season –
grown man barefoot all summer long,
and mules for the freeze all winter.
Work is the crocus sack, stained
with dung and sweat, smacking your back,
filled with cotton. Work is the day
you think you are grown enough
to run, to stop this constant stepping back,
only to find that big-bellied white man
with his straw hat, overalls, cigar
in his mouth and black-as-night shades,
with a shotgun in his hand saying,
"Here are some stripes, nigger,
nice stripes to help you work better.
Now you get three meals a day, uncle;
now you get a bed to sleep on, boy;
now you got something to live for."
Work is the time you spend trying to eat away
the time you owe; work is all a nigger has
for sure, and work tells you that nobody,
nobody is going to give you something
for nothing. Work is like breathing,
but after a while there is no more
breathing left, and every breath
is a loan, and your pocket is empty,
and you will never pay it back. Work is all
a man has, and work is nothing,
nothing at all; work, work, work, work…

THE FAVOUR OF POLITICIANS

Never let a politician grant you a favour
They will always want to
Control you forever.
                    —Bob Marley

i

I have never trusted what politicians say; it's no random
judgement on them, but what you learn when the music
of your early days is the music of treachery that leads
to long knives, to executions on the beach, to the mornings
when your stomach is heavy with a kind of sorrow
that makes you void with no easy explanation –
something like the fear a child feels when his parents
quarrel, the dark heaviness in the air, the knowledge
that people die, that kingdoms come and kingdoms go,
that the sound of martial music over the airwaves
signals a new pretender animated with the hope
of power, but destined to be a stiff, mute face, squalid
with drying blood, the way photographs of the dead
are still on the pages of newspapers.

In Jamaica, I understood at once Marley's
quiet advice on politicians granting favours
and controlling you forever. I'd seen how casually
the blunt power of threats had arrived at our door
after Neville's death, and I, heavy with the necessary gall,
had worked out the logic of his death as a kind of murder,
the way the state slaughters its thinkers, those who offer
challenges, and the relentlessness of vindictiveness,
so when the Maximum Leader offered me work,
a gift, it became a test, which in the hands of a politician
is a threat. I wish I could say I stood my ground,
but my mother, still heavy with her mourning, weary of the wars,
told me to act wisely, do it, do it, do it, so I did.

I tell this story to my daughter, a confession,
a lesson: the advice that sometimes he who fights
and runs away, lives to fight another day, that somewhere
in every heroic arc is the coward's chapter, that low
point of it all. To hear this is a comfort, she says,
in her own wars, the battles she sees before her,
here in this world of dead presidents, dead heroes,
dead soldiers, of lies told for the sake of lies,
of the lies leaders tell to make the world bow to them,
of tyrant women who wave their hands for the thug
to swing the machete, because she, too, understands
that power is a fleeting thing. Now, with dark conspiracies
in rooms like our living room, with uncles and cousins
in prison, with the uncertainty of tomorrow and tomorrow,
I am never surprised by the machinations of power.
It's a sickness that crept into my body through the blood
of those who bloodied me, from the betrayals that marked
my ancestry in the world – in the crossing of seas,
in the walk through the woods only to be taken away,
in the ways in which all power over the weak
is built on lies, and the helicopter thumping in the air
is the arrival of another lie. So, these days, I seek
a language to empathize with those who have been wounded
by these times, been shattered, betrayed, tricked, blackmailed,
through perjury, cover-ups, undercover surveillance,
coups, destabilization: this is the constant anthem
of my memory, and my daily existence is built
on holding firm to beauty: the playwright filling a stage
with a storm of truth, the shattering of all lies.
This in the music of metaphor, the honesty of the metaphor
in the vulnerability of story, in the art that risks everything.
This is the world I have always known, not cynicism but
an understanding that all patriotism is as fickle as
cheering for a football team and rejoicing for days.

This is as far as it goes. We make our own path
from day to day, knowing that maybe faith
is the buttress against the noise; it is for me.

iii

When I stand on the street and look at the tall, narrow face
of the six-storey, 1900, flat-iron building that's at its end,
with its dark iron balustrades and a veneer
the colour of pale tanned leather, see the shadows
where the windows look out, and the elegant lines
of the boulevard (in which the building is a kind of island)
that stretch back deep into the city, a monument
of hubris and power, something that stands, I suppose,
like an eighteenth-century galleon might have stood
at the docks, startling those who came near the water
with its overwhelming size, the grace of its woodwork,
a vessel that carried commerce and trade. Yet, staring
at this act of power, I know the only lasting thing
about this vision is the sky behind, grey and morose,
streaked with white clouds, the backdrop that will remain
even when this building, too, collapses, and I wonder
at the rumble in the distance – a storm or bombs.

ON HEARING NEWS OF ANOTHER BLACK MAN SHOT

I ask you for the lemon-green room, the room
where colour enfolds, leaving a soft
and comforting green over the worn
books and discarded folders. Let me describe
this green as the light filtering through
the shade of leaves. Imagine a bowl
of green olives or grapes in their variable
shades: this is the green I'm thinking of,
or a green that's settled after an explosion,
or the multi-voiced shades of my island.
I must be clear about this, for green
is as fickle as the bodies we live in.
I'll sit there, dappled, as if there are trees
filtering light over me. Over there a lime tree,
stunted by the entanglement of its roots
in the pot, smiles sheepishly in the corner.
How addictive is the green shade that
covers me now; without it, I become
a creature shuddering for the caress
of tender light. I am feeling the news,
the chattering noises, the illogic
of another black body broken by bullets,
by the heaviest of sorrows.
Forgive me, friend, for asking you to take me
into your verdant backroom. Forgive me
if I sit quietly in the corner rocking, hoping, maybe,
for earth to hold steady my vegetable self.

AGAINST ERASURE

i

By what obscene delusion
are we turning erasure
into an art, we the silenced
and erased ones,
we the descendants
of those whose records
were stolen?

Why, instead, should we not
write, as keepers
of history in our art,
such lines as,

"On such-and-such a date
I found in such-and-such a desk
of such-and-such a general
the truth of my ancestors in ledgers,
in ink and in songs and symbols
and stamps and bones"?

Why should we not feed
the silence with our songs
instead of this collusion
with our disappearances?

ii

Every poet should long
for the particular dusk
when a stranger wearing
a tailored suit and beads
arrives at their gate

with a portmanteau
choking with sheets
of paper, documents,
deeds, yellowing folders
falling apart, a clump
of rubber stained with lead,
and a bottle of Indian ink —
aged effects with the look
of things carelessly
left behind.

iii

The stranger says to the poet,
"I know nothing of poetry
but I know you are
the chroniclers
of the heart; I know
you are spies who slip
under cover of darkness
into the fortified cities
and collect the dreams
of the living and the dead.
I know that it is not
the winners who garland history
but the poets; they defy
the callous disregard
of blood; I want you
to look at these, study
them, and then dream
or have hauntings,
and then chronicle
the things you see."

iv

Every poet desires
the command
of a prophetess,
not in a dream
but real as open wounds
across a hand,
who says *Go!*
and they must go
to vouchsafe the memory
of the broken earth
before it vanishes;
or retrieve from the deep
silence of the family
the voices silenced
by the comfort of forgetting,
for the quiet are not
always voiceless,
they have just chosen
to forget, for forgetting
is more livable.

v

The poet is offered nothing in return,
no garland, no coin, just the earnestness
of the woman who says, "This is the last time
I may be able to do this", between long draughts
of cigarette smoke and a rattling cough.
She offers only the safe passage that comes
with a people who have, despite it all,
learned to value the keeper of words,
the singer and seer, who will offer a meal,
a bed to rest on and warnings in the face of danger.

vi

This is the thing all poets must crave;
otherwise, what are they for, these words,
words, wormwood and words,
the fatigue of words, the indulgence of words
the hollow womb of words?

vii

On the corner opposite the stadium's parking lot
squats the brick Arts building that reeks of gas seeping
into the chilled air, a warning of sudden explosion,
and, monthly, the sirens crowd the air as red, yellow
and blue neon lights brighten the streets around it.

On my daily walks I imagine what the messenger-woman,
in her tailored suit and dreadlocks from the far-off country,
with the heavy accent of molasses and carved wood,
speaks of what she sees or dreams as she moves
through her apocalypse, the things that make her say:
"I must find a poet to tell this, and when the poet writes this
I can die knowing I have done something."

viii

All poets need to see a painting
of indecipherable shapes and strokes
that makes them feel the deep dampness
of sorrow, that causes them to discern
in the chaos a galleon's sail,
a clamorous ocean, the hint of bodies thrashing
and reaching for the light, and maybe this is how
we understand the songs we make.

IV

...I close my eyes to push/ away the darting lights...

LOS OJOS DEL MUNDO

Those who live under mountains look from birth
for the shelter of trees, for large cathedrals, grand
edifices holy for their size, awesome
for the manner in which they dwarf us, make
us think of the smallness of our lives.
Those who walk along stony paths that follow
a river's grand drama of monumental motion
know the muscular swoop of its current
bearing all the country's collected waters,
every drop contained in the deep channel
it cuts in the earth. Those of us who are
deafened by the clamour of the river
understand God, understand what it means
to hurl the frail, delicate morsel of a vestal virgin
into the current, feeding the grandeur
of the cosmos. Those who know the spray of rain,
the great laughter of a storm pouring from
the mountainous sky, know that this body
we have been given, so impolitely fragile,
is our only tool, our only power.
We know the miracle of our bodies'
monstrous engineering; we know that sheltered
like this, our eyes, staring out of flesh's
swaddling, our cocoon, carry the universe,
can subdue the mountains, contain the swollen
river, build grand cathedrals and let them fall
to rubble. This is what remains – the open
stare of a girl leaning against a wall,
draped in the warmth of her secrets.

CATHEDRAL

When my soul was hurtin' deep within,
And I'm worrying to be free, desperately, yeah
— Bob Marley "Give Thanks and Praises"

After "Cathedral" from *Subterranea* by Sally Gall

i

The note, scribbled on a piece of stained tissue,
rough with slivers of unprocessed pulp,
simply read: "You believe you are interesting;
it is a lie." This truth we uncover in the dark grotto
of a cathedral's high walls and looming avenues.
Imagine a commissioned artist building
a contraption to lift his aching bones
for his last great duty, to create the art
that will outlast generations. Imagine this
as the first view of the task ahead – this artist
mapping the contours of the uneven walls,
composing a stomach, a nipple, an eye socket,
a blade of grass, a pool of stagnant water,
against the markings of nature – the lumpiness
of stone, the way light falls to the ground.

In this subterranean space, think of a healed wound,
an open mouth, a bowl for aromatic leaves
and petals, twigs and precious stones,
of the perfect revelatory moment while praying
in this shadow hall, carved out by centuries
of flood waters. I know there is no beauty
in my expressions of holiness or my glowing face
coming from the mountain top;
that every whisper of adoration is a
cesspool of insecurity; that a good night's

sleep – empty of dreams – is as clear a truth
as there ever will be. To know this is
to understand that nothing is assured.
I let out a gut-wrenching howl. The echo
continues for as long as I dare listen.

ii

I will build a cathedral to dwarf my worries,
the grand arches free of fine details, without
sculpture that replicates our human fretting.
This black cavern of such imposing grandeur
will consume even the cry of my lamentation.
So, when I raise my voice to the heights, echoing
double and treble, my voice will follow
the curl of incense into the dark void above.
This crescendo of stone, this elevation
of the final dreams, the revelator speaking
in the pure abandon of the future tense,
this noise of stone on stone will be a temple
so stunning it will shatter doubt,
swallow uncertainty – will be my Amen.
So be it, so be it, and so be it.

POST-ELEGY

*Elegies are one of the few places where we can do the work of care,
not just to ourselves but to our dead...*
— Romeo Oriogun

Evening, and my dead sister does not reply;
she is more tutored in the language of prayer.
The empty streets, the honking geese, the soft light
of dusk are still my cloister. I pace, and the slow
thaw of mourning starts again. It's been
three years, and my satchel overflows with news,
the thickening of words cramped in my chest
until the long heaviness of what's unspoken
begins to untangle: the news, the confessions,
the laughter, the shadow of the long silence of the plague.

I live in another country. The place where her bones rest
is nostalgic to me. For too long, I have not visited
that sun-beaten patch of earth to stand mute,
then speak for want of doing something better.
My mourning has been starved and the gift
of the chattering dead taken from me.
So, here I am, mouth moving, building a shrine
for tomorrow, the tongues we all must speak,
someday, soon. It helps to know this in the silence
that returns, and the warmth that envelopes me.
It is true what Oriogun said, that what I long
for is the gift of caring for the dying,
and now the grace of caring for the dead.

HOW I PRAY IN THE PLAGUE

I was rehearsing the ecstasies of starvation
for what I had to do. And have not charity,
I found my pity, desperately researching
the origins of history, from reed-built communes
by sacred lakes, turning with the first sprocketed
water-driven wheels.
— Derek Walcott

In these silences, the bubbles of hurt
are indistinguishable from the terror
that lurks in the body. The phrase "ecstasies of
starvation" has a music that lures us to peace,
but how do I stay with a tender heart
and calm in the face of an old saying
that hides its conundrum of theology
from me – perhaps not hides, perhaps
what I mean is that before I found pity,
charity and love, I was faced by the conundrum,
lead me not into temptation – that imperative
that has no sensible meaning. For is this
the way of a father? What kind of father
must be asked not to tempt us? And what of
the diabolical cruelty of such testing?
If I'd said, "Neville, please, lead me not
into temptation", what would that have meant?
Would it not have been a reprimand to my father,
a judgment on his propensity to fail me?
You see why I need to slip over this with a faith
that needs to grow in increments
of meaning? In these silences, the bubbles
of anxiety that I cannot distinguish
from terror is my daily state. You teach
me to pray in this way, and in this way,
you offer me the path that leads to terror.

And what of the way of poetry to change
the words of this small conundrum:
"Lead us not, lead me not, lead them not"?
What is this if not an attempt to evade the heavy
hand of God? For if to pray "Lead *them* not
into temptation" displays a kind of mercy,
to say, "Lead *us* not", though it seems
the penitence of a sinning nation desperate
for the lifting of the curses of contagion and plague,
its subtext is the finger pointed at the culprit.
So what kind of father is this? Do you want answers?
You have come to the wrong place.
I am selfish with answers. I am hoarding them.
Go, instead, to the prophets, the preachers,
the soothsayers, the pundits and dream readers,
the pontiffs and kings, the presidents and imams,
all the brokers in answers. As for me, I will hoard
the calming beauty of these puzzles and walk
this road, not as the demander of absolute clarity,
but with the fabric of uncertainty stretched
as a net across the afternoon sky.
Under this I will journey until all music ends,
and the air grows dry as a lack of grace.

They say that if you find honey in the stomach
of the baobab tree, you must leave
the better part for the spirit of the tree,
and then share the remnant sweetness
with your neighbours. What you hear
among the reeds, in the arms of the trees,
in the shelter of the sky, that is enough
for the days of terror and sorrow.
Amen.

MAKING A DEAL

God, it seems, won't make such a deal; it is
not always clear why this is. The devil,
though, loiters at the railroad tracks cutting through
the abandoned back streets of southern towns,
waiting for a middling talent to come by.
The devil traffics in souls, and it's an easy sale
when the talent stops to contemplate it:
he has a dollar in his pocket, a thumb length
of whiskey in his flask, and his horn
or guitar or harmonica or fiddle is all
he has that he can put a price on.
His soul is mostly a word somebody told him
about in church or in the Gospel Home
where the soup is a little salty and thin
but always hot, and the bread freshly baked
and sweet. But he has never seen his soul,
never touched it, never smelled it,
never tasted it, even though, they say,
it is somewhere inside him. How to reason
if it was his to buy or sell in the first place,
when he can't be sure if he has one?
Now his penis, he can look at; it grows
and shrinks, it fills his hand; it winks
at him, it breathes, and a lot of women say
they can feel it when it presses in.
Now cut that off, and a man has lost
something he knows he used to have –
a piece of him is gone. But the soul,
well, is it like this thing in him
that makes him know when the sound
he makes is right, that can make people say,
You got it! Can it be bought or sold, held up,
rubbed up against, beat down?
Maybe the two things are the same.

So when the devil, picking his teeth
in the hot sun, boots shining like a new penny,
looks the man in the eyes and says,
"Give me your soul and I will give you talent,
more talent than you know what to do with" –
well, somebody is pulling a fast one,
somebody's getting a better deal
than somebody else – somebody is a sucker,
and somebody is not. The man knows
that if he can do a deal with the devil,
then he is going to hell anyway,
so all he's got is now, and now is big
as the sky and the world of good times
and power, Florsheim shoes and a tailored suit.
The deal is easy: nothing for nothing and the music
is sweet over the dry-backed southern town.

WHEN WE PRAY

When we pray – that earnest gesture
of eyes closed so tight we see the bright
darting of spirits, shatterings of gold
and red, and after a while no longer
hear the soft hiccups in the closed
room – when we ask that this stone
sitting upon us will pass, that this
rotting will pass, that this confounding
bewilderment will pass, these are ways
to stand in the shadows and see through
the dark maw to the refuge ahead, to shut
away the demons, to know that when
the eyes open it will be dawn and all
the wounded ones will have walked away.
I pass on to you the secrets I find
too weighty for my satchel; I pass on to you,
on the wings of prophesy, the stones
the stranger placed at my door;
I pass on to you in the sermon's fire
the burdens I will not carry. This is how
I lighten my load, and how I can walk
through the looming gloom ahead of me.
I am the author of my shame,
the wounded and the worried, and I close
my eyes to push away the darting lights
speeding toward my centre.

FAITH HEALING

In the glaring light, the question is unfortunate,
now that you are breathing slowly, now you have cooled
as after orgasm, your body emptied of tension
– that war to arrive at the riotous hallelujah –
and there's a dull thumping in your head, your eyes
downcast in the moment of embarrassment
after abandon and dance; and the crowd's become
ordinary again, blank faces searching memory
for where the car is parked; and the musicians,
pimple-faced journeymen, are gathering up their leads;
and the blue carpet has lost its sheen – the waves
you saw, the surf undulating, the shimmering of sunlight;
and the rafters look bare, the glare of fluorescents
flattening everything – a temple returned to a gym –
you can smell the sweat; so now, when she asks,
"Are you healed? Was it something you can tell?"
you know this too young counsellor is not a prophetess.
"It is in my blood." "Ah." The eyes remain blank.
When the preacher and healer were high-stepping
amens around your fallen quivering self –
you dreaming of arriving at the water's edge
and finding only stones – and the voice was saying,
"Where is the water, why did you take all the water?"
and you cried at this, which the preacher said unleashed
forgiveness, and then came the blows of his voice,
"Out! Out! Out!" before music gathered
and he was gone, the lingering scent of lemons
and sugar in his wake. "It's in my blood…"
you repeat, and she pleads with damp eyes,
Don't tell me, don't tell me, don't tell me.
And you don't say the words dancing wildly
in your skull; you don't say them out of mercy,
out of a strange, embarrassed kind of grace.

UNDERTAKER AT THE VILLAGE CEMETERY

On a chill morning, it's forgivable
for the walker passing the village cemetery,
its graves like bivouacs scattered about
the uneven field, with its shacks of cheap balsam
and raffia roofs, to imagine the heavy mist
moving through the madrugada to be
the steaming expiation of the freshly
buried dead, as if in this cool dawn, the days
of waiting have passed for sacrifices
to be made, fears shed, farewells uttered
and all forgiveness granted, and the spirits
are now rising into the open sky,
because even a stranger knows that the sweet
earthen stench of decay that seems to stick
to the skin is the residue left behind
while the pure white mist uncurling around
the listing crucifixes is the holy essence
of all the living. The walker will wave
to the undertaker who nods, picking his way
through the site, making his path to the new
shelter he is digging, as the oppression
of sunlight dries up this holy silence.

DECUBITUS IN FIVE FRAMES

After Santiago Carbonell's *La Persistencia de la Pintura*

1

After the Rebels

"It was as if Death," she said, "halted us.
You came to find me, but you don't
want to look. This is it." She took up
the photo of the long, tree-lined boulevard,
the one that connected the grand mansions,
now gutted, their white walls black with soot.
In the photograph, the man was dressed
in a black tweed suit, a tailored shirt,
still brilliant white in spots. And though
the fabric was rent, stained in parts with blood,
one could see how it ended, his legs
thrown apart, his arms wide open
with the kind of resignation that followed
the crossed arms of self-protection – as if to say,
Okay, okay, I resign my body to you.
The crows had been there, and the skull,
for that is what it was, despite the killing
happening only a week before,
was nearly detached and bare of flesh,
but filthy like something you wrap
in a garbage bag and discard. The crows
had chosen the head, easily reached,
with none of the distraction of frozen cloth.
She said, smoking, "I took the photo so that,
late at night in the dark room I would see
that what he rested on was not a shadow,
but his residue, a kind of afterlife,
the thing that will remain on the cobbled ground
long after he was lifted onto the cart,
and taken to the open fields of his estate."

2

Fantasy

Inside us lives a desire for a drafty hall
built for those monstrous machines that old
industries thrived on – those steel sculptures
that dwarfed workers who moved in slow
ritual each day to be consumed by steam
and metallic poisons. Now these halls,
emptied of all their groaning engines,
are as silent as the dreams of radio hosts
who talk and talk each coin they pocket
into being. My desire is to own such a place,
with a high strip of smoke-yellowed windows
through which brilliant unforgiving light
makes gold the stripped flooring.
Here, I'll arrive with others, as if called
by the factory's siren, to labour on our art.
Inside, we are heavy-booted, bearded by neglect,
funky-smelling, coffee-soaked creators
of the last testaments of light, people who
disappear for days, makers of beauty who fall
asleep in wheelbarrows, hands clutching
a still drying bush, the soft light of morning
opening out like a pool of piss around us,
great artists in repose, bodies fatigued
by that final expenditure of passion, dead to the world,
dead to the anxiety that what we have made
is fit for the dump, dead to fear; dead
to the quarrels causing our families
to contemplate a time when we will be dead.

3
Naked

The body that poses for the repeated
artist's hand conceals its own myths,
like how long can one clench muscles
to create the taut stoniness of a hard self?
After twenty minutes, it's impossible,
something will loosen in the thighs and stomach,
and the body, seeking light, will let
the slow eyes of the sun settle on every
secret within us. Our imperfect selves
will retreat, pimpled and spotted,
with blotches and flesh flopping on flesh,
into a dark room, our faces staring into the gloom,
until we learn our greatest healing comes
with nakedness, with the body unadorned,
being everything it is and nothing more.
This is what we should know as beautiful,
the body as the final truth, the way
that at last everything relaxes, and we
can see that water is the language of all flesh,
that what glows in this world is the final act
of defiance before we succumb to sleep,
or even death. My envy of your prone,
freely-naked self, foolish, no doubt,
still it stays with me when I speak to you
as the ocean speaks to the wide-open sky.

4

How the Monk Conjures Sleep

For sleep, the monk made haunting music
with his fingers, rising with the scent of linseed
from the upright piano – chords complicating
themselves in declensions and sweet distortions.
To avoid the hot early morning dreams
of the halls of gin and whiskey, the monk
would pray, "Remember, Lord the safety
of man and of beast, and of me, thy sinful
servant." Sometimes he would cry until his face
was wet with tears. For sleep, the monk
would gather his brown cassock and dream
of the vestibule where the font of holy water
shone in the muted light. Once, he followed
the sound of a voice, big with mellow aromas,
through the chapel, singing, "The Bible tells so."
There he found her, head thrown back,
her voice full as a mountain, and she turned,
caught him there, stared at him, still singing,
until he knew she could see the shame on his face.
She smiled, triumphant huntress, so all he could say
was "You are… you are… a woman!", with awe,
such holy awe, and then they both laughed a pure, full laugh
as if they both knew that desire can be as holy
as prayer. For sleep, the monk carried next to his skin,
the calming pebbles of a riverside, where a host
of migrants sat around a dark, fire-blackened tin
filled with beans, and before eating they said
a prayer for the golden evening light, and he could feel
the power in the foreheads of the harbourless wanderers
land in the palms of his hands. For sleep, the monk
now always thinks of the woman sitting among
the stragglers singing, and how she stopped and looked
at him saying, "You do things a beautiful way."

5
Balm in Gilead

In Sandy Gut, St. Catherine, a gloomy cottage stands
at the foothills of the grand mountains that swallowed slaves;
it's where my wife's ancestress walked barefoot
all her life, her soles calloused to a hardened armour –
her toes, pliable as fingers, could grip stones
and shatter pieces of wood. She climbed
coconut trees well into her seventies, her skirt's hem
hitched into her waist, her legs sinuous, rippling
with efficiency. Descending quickly, she panted briefly
as if to cover the shame of gawkers, quickly peeling
away the copra with a machete to find the seed.
Those hands gathered bush, calling their names
as if praying. I fantasize her voice saying, "Okay, ready,"
with that gentle impatience that is a blood trait
my wife has inherited. I enter the gloom,
see the mist rising up from the porcelain bath
set there in the middle of the dirt floor. She nods
to the stool. I sit. "But wait, how you can bade like so."
The teeth hiss, rolling into a deep belly chuckle.
I strip. She turns and squats before me, takes my feet
in her hands with rough assuredness and, with a rag,
she cleans the decades of wayward and unrighteous paths
I have walked, cleans all falsehoods, myths, betrayals,
all acts of foolishness – decades of them. She stands
and I know to enter the water, bare as I am,
the thick scent of mint and astringent green
overwhelming me. Her voice, her breath,
her prayers, her patience, her sweat, her hands,
yes, her hands of command are laid on me
until I fall into a stupor – the comfort of ritual,
the healing I have longed for.

HORNS

In every crowd, there is the one
with horns, casually moving through
the bodies as if this is the living

room of a creature with horns,
a long cloak and the song of tongues
on the lips of the body. To see

the horns, one's heart rate must
reach one hundred and seventy-
five beats per minute, at a rate

faster than the blink of an eye,
for the body with horns lives
in the space between the blink

and light. Slow down the blink
and somewhere in the white space
between sight and sightlessness

is twilight, and in that place,
that gap, the stop-time, the horn-
headed creature appears,

spinning, dancing, strolling
through the crowd; and in the fever
of revelation, you will

understand why the shaman
is filled with the hubris
of creation, why the healer

forgets herself and feels like
an angel about to take flight.
My head throbs under

the mosquito mesh, the drums
do not stop through the night,
the one with horns feeds

me sour porridge and nuts
and sways, *Welcome, welcome*.

THE BODY
After "Skylark" by Brian Rutenberg

The monster walks toward the mud
of the vanishing light, the voices whispering
approbation through the night and,
curled up on himself, the monster asks
his penis questions that have no answers.
You are, he says, the gun that turned into a straw.
You are the betrayer of all my silences.
You are a storm of delight. You are to be bled,
drained until you shrink, until you are a dry whisp
of mummified flesh. If you take a whip
and turn a body into pulp, and if the body
does not have the strength to stop the whip,
then no one will call that body strong,
no one will see that body shine. If you take
a hand, and force it inside that body, twist
a flame of pain deep inside that body,
and apart from a dull whimper of protest,
the body does not know how to fight back,
no one will call that body fierce, no one will
say that body has grace. Deep in the mud,
curled up with the percolation of bitterness,
steeped in the marinate of shame, the body
grows a callus thick as a hundred years of lament.
At dawn, see it coming towards you in the half light –
this is the barnacled weapon of our defiance,
this is the monstrous body of wars and wars,
broken for you, broken for you.
Take, eat…

THE REMNANT

i

Debris, like the scattering of bones
on the seabed, coral growing around
the long history of bodies jettisoned –
this is a myth the artist must
imagine as a biblical calamity.

The truth is that sand will cover
all evidence, and the ancestors
singing deep in the ocean won't
be heard. Soon, in the soft rumble
of walls of moving water,
deafness will be all that is left.

ii

Beneath the freeway – now empty
of all vehicles – the pillars that hold
up the interlocking maze of asphalt
and cement is the graveyard of all desire.
We walk among the broken planks,
the empty cars, the tattered garments,
and there find ourselves alone,
the wind moving with the constant hum
of air circling the void.

To hold ourselves intact, we must
close our eyes and imagine green,
and then, for sustenance, drag our
tongues across each other's foreheads,
to taste the salt and sweet of our hope.

WASHING WOMEN

When, deep in the afternoon,
the children, drunk with laughter
and fatigue, have fallen on their backs
and are gazing sleepily into sky,
following the slow drift of light clouds;
and the clothes are growing warm
on the rocks, heated to a dark dryness
by the sun; when the women know
the men are still a half hour away,
and they slip off their sweat-heavy blouses
and brassieres to soak them in the last
of the soapy water, and rub fabric
on fabric, their bodies warming
against the soft hand of the afternoon sun;
the gentle caress of the bridge's shadow,
wooden and elegant above the river,
blesses them like a healer touches
the body of one who's sick, who's been
waiting on the sideroads for the shadow
of the saint to touch them for an instant,
for the power to come upon them,
to heal them, and fire in them the grace
of love as it roams the world.

THE DARKEST ELATION

This is the darkest elation,
the moment when all walls are breached,
the instant when the wind
rushes into the hungry crevices,
porticos, hovels and deep courtyards.
In that moment, we bask
in the sweetest surrender. Tears
and deep shudders overwhelm us,
the air waiting with held breath
for the tender aftermath.
The body understands
the bruises that will darken
on it, and welcomes
the darkest elation there is.

STRUGGLE, ESCAPE, ECSTASY

i

It's been months and all I hear is quietness,
the silence of reluctant memory. Time
resists the urge to recall. I want to express
sorrow though I don't know the wound to rhyme.
At forty-two, the shape of my life was ritual:
failures and delight, and both were tempered
by the children growing, a mercy for someone
who understood that a moth is a creature
of despair. I welcomed love's escape,
I sang, *The cancer's gone, so now comes ecstasy.*

ii

Before the cancer, shocks and terrors
had been kept at bay. *Go on, go on,*
the body shouted. We were endeared
to the rugged life of exile, each stone
hoisted up the stairs and planted: the leave-
and-come-again our pattern until the bare
earth remained. Our triumph was sealed with a kiss.
Then, the alarm came, the start of our grief –
two years of labouring to hold in all bliss.
Then, we breathed, watchful as the skies cleared.

MIST

I am a graveyard.
Here, there is no mourning;
the dead are dumb as wood.

I have forgotten how to cry
because I can see spirits,
as if the graves have broken

open on this red
resurrection morning.
The earth is a mansion

with many floors,
the layering of centuries,
the spirits strolling

across the world's plains;
so many millions
gone, only to return

as if there are many
earths transparent
as the glassy film

of ice over a pond.
I don't know names
anymore; spirits

is what we call them;
they travel as soft
as clouds or mist.

These days, I stand
before a boiling pot
until it dries and cracks,

all the steam
caressing me like the love
of the dead.

I am a graveyard
wet with sea fog.
My memories

will not let me go.
I am staring upwards
looking for blue

sky through
the crowd of souls
streaking across the heavens.

LIGHT HOME

Build me a house of light,
stretches of emptiness glaring
into an open sky, calling
the colours in, but mostly
the white light that consumes
shadows, that turns this body
of riverbed brown into something
transparent like an ochre-
coloured piece of cotton flapping
in the air. Build me a house
of new light, the daily whisper
of dialects crawling across
the cedar and tamarind
woods; build me a house
where the rain beads the glass
panes over us, the fragile
membrane separating
us from the chaos
of the other side. Furnish
our cabin with the white
and sepia brown of things,
the dull pewter of ancient
lead, the gleam of decanters,
hundreds of them, lining
the walls. Build me
a house for my musty
eyes, a house where
faces, illuminated, reveal
themselves to be as familiar
as a plain book of poems
opened out – call it splayed –
on the table, my desk,
the scene of such terrible crimes.

V

. . . Build me a house of light. . .

ODE TO THE CLOTHESLINE
After Alfred Stieglitz

If minor in the missing of things gone,
there's nostalgia for the colours, the music,

the revelation of a family's ordinary life
caught in the flap and dance, the jig

of layers, of outer and inner skins,
the secret things so close to the body,

the salt and sweet of blood and shit
and piss, scrubbed then rinsed, leaving

beneath the astringent scent of soap
a musky marker of selves for strays

to smell or imagine as they inspect
the parade of the absent living,

hung on taut lines, propped by poles with nails
for a hook, above the startling green of grass

and hedge, the barefaced concrete steps,
and beyond the sky, inscrutable as a wall.

What one takes away as a kind of sweetness
is the labour of brown hands, elbow-deep in suds,

the rituals of cleansing, the humility of darns
or a frayed crotch, the dignity of cleanliness,

the democracy of truth,
the way we lived our lives in the open.

THE MATHEMATICIAN

The limestone wall is the canvas on which
the mathematician writes his theorems
deep in the night, on his way home from the sea
in the shadow and light of the beach fire.
He wears a fedora, a white doctor's coat,
the shorts of a Bermuda policeman, circa
1958, and a Marley T-shirt, one he wore
as a teenager – twenty years on and it
still holds the colour. Always his compass,
divider, triangle and square ruler; always
the chalk and charcoal. This madness of numbers
and letters and symbols grows across
the white surface of the cathedral wall
like the score of a mento tune, and no one
dares to touch it; they leave it until rain
clears away the magic, until the ground sucks
up the incantation of the stars, which
is what he calls them. We all long to be
known for something, to be given a nickname
that others will know; to be, even for
an instant, present in this world.

THREE LATTER-DAY DUPPIES

One moves with familiar ease down the slope.
The second wears a loose, casual suit. He has three
in his cupboard that he rotates – grey, nondescript,
and threadbare at the collars. The third has money
or pretends to have money; he has no job ahead
of him. His is a body moving through its own
city like a tourist; he will sit in the courtyard
of the gallery, eat a meat patty, drink paper cups
of coffee, and smoke, waiting for his lover
to come from her daily work, each day a ritual
of adventures.
              The first moves with familiar
ease down the slope to the drought-dry garden.
From there, he sees the silhouettes of bodies
on the slanting stairs, the wall of the great
stadium stained with the residue of algae
on carbon, the stain of the apocalypse –
what we are told will remain after the fire.

The city has been growing out of the forests
for centuries, perpetually at war
with fecundity and decay – the inhabitants,
constantly aware that if we don't mind
sharp, the forest will consume it all.
So we come and go each morning,
relieved to see that the street cleaners
have kept the voracious green at bay,
though at the gravesides of our dead, we say,
"Return to what made you, return to green,
return to moss." Tomorrow, we fear
that the news will come of the chaos of
a collapsing government, and the debris
of our unwashed, neglected city
will be scattered about the streets,

and rumours of revolution in the heavy scent
of burning tires will fill the air, though "Revolution"
is too organised a word for what we fear.

This is how a city dies, how a state fails,
how we the people move back and forth,
like those three latter-day duppies:
one casual as another day in the interim between
hope and calamity; the second sniffing his armpits
to smell his rot and the stink of prophecy on his body;
while the third, smoking, smoking, slowly,
calmly, contemplates the end of pleasure.

THE REUNION

JoAnne, you remember the last meeting before her death
that November? Jamaica had lost its petulance;
the season of sorrel, rum and bloody poinsettias
was gathering strength, and in that hiatus,
in a house buried by trees, in the hills overlooking
the sea, people whispered and laughed. She
was there, her skin warm with chocolate smoothness,
her hair alarmingly white, heavy coils of plaits
falling about her. You talked of remembering,
but it was as if you were both forgetting the wounds,
the skin covered with fire ants, the long chasm
between you, the decades of sowing silence.
So, you asked for two secrets, and she promised
a third after your two. "I hated you for a long time,"
she said. "And I painted you as a fat monstrosity, full
of pomposity and bile. This stopped three years
ago when I met your son; he said you sent your love."
The second: "For thirty days I have fasted on lime juice
and scotch bonnet peppers so I could look beautiful.
I bought this dress for you. See my back, the muscles —
look!" You told her that for years you dreamed
of a winter week, snowed in, and both of you
walking through the halls of your home of glass,
the room heated to 80 degrees — both of you naked,
you painting canvases. "Was I as we were then?"
she asked. "No," you said. "We were both as we are
and beautiful, and my paintings were of
our new bodies, blue and wrinkled and graceful
and guiltless before the fall. I have never hated you.
I have only feared you." Both of you smiled. Then she said,
"I am dying." And she did. It was only a month.
You heard in January, on a slate-grey day,
the ground covered with three-day-old snow.
You painted her back as if her hands were bound

at the wrist, and you wept with the memory
of what was lost. There is always, at the fore
of all beauty, the falseness of art that treats our bodies,
as if we were ever anything other than pimpled,
sweaty, smelly pieces of meat, waiting valiantly
for the moment we give up and start to rot.

RAIN

For Claude Clarke

Oh, to live in a world of giant leaves,
big as sheets, so that when the storms come,
as they always will, a barefoot man
won't have to worry about
messing his clothes up with wet,
and a one-panty woman
won't have to worry about
the kink rushing back into her good
hot-combed hair, for she and he
could find shelter in the ordinary
miracle of those big-bodied leaves,
taller than a grown woman,
wider than a grown man,
just laying around in the world,
waiting.

ON BECOMING

The painting is of a door, its wood so warped
with moisture it stays ajar, leaving a sliver of light —

enough to suggest something sweet
and almost unreachable behind the door.

You sit in your room working on the bills
or those comforting lists that make you believe

you have finally multiplied time, made wide open spaces
of emptiness you are free to use or not use;

but you keep looking at that gap, keep peering in,
trying to see what is there, and occasionally you get up

and touch it, as if you might feel what is there.
I am being coy. I am not talking about you,

but about me. And it is not a door, but a painting
of a naked woman sitting like a pear on a perch,

her knees drawn up to her chest, her head buried
between her knees, her feet touching,

and the shadow between her shins and her thighs
whispering flesh. The fingers of her left hand carry

the string of a yoyo, bouncing like a sandwich pushcart
below her toes. That is the only thing that moves

on this woman whose silence, the silence
of her body, is what moves me to speak.

THE UNSPEAKABLE THINGS

From the ocean's edge, the land rises against
a sky of subtle colours. The ground
beyond the thin lip of beach is a grand
scattering of stones, as if a massive blow
of a giant hammer, or God's hand,
smashed into a broad slab of brown granite,
leaving the broken shards where they have settled.
There is no green here, just this endless stretch
of stone. This ground feels stable, but love
gives no assurances. A Chinese poet
writes that love is not in pleasure or desire,
but in something that smells as safe
as kindness. The wind is picking up
here. When someone, safe as a grandmother, embraces you and says, "My heart
is so full of love for you, so full,"
is this not the purity of desire, the thing
that carries every orgasm, every laugh,
every gloomy dawn, every lonely week
of wondering, every elegy, every
bewilderment of a child's body breaking,
every blow to her heart and skin, and this
soft whispering of the cancer multiplying?
The truest things are broken, shattered plates
of ancient rock still there in the cold dawn light.
That is the love we have no language for.

AFTER THE BIOPSY

She weighs her joy and finds it wanting,
her body now a conundrum of betrayals.
How easily we forget how the nail
gently brushing a nipple sends light,
oh, the bright light of the world, piercing
through our bodies, spreading the irritable
sweetness of delight and needle pricks.
Now, cupped, her breasts carry the weight
of all her fears; the nipples have grown
into wounds, a warning where used to be pleasure.
These days it is hard not to know that left alone,
untouched, the body returns to a native smell,
the smell of earth, of decay, of corruption,
and this is a testing of faith. We wait for
our Charon to arrive in a lab coat, with hands
smelling of antiseptic creams. No one has
to prophesy death, the bones pushing against
the skin; here is where they say her end begins,
this purple spot, this complex of dark veins
and stone-hard flesh, this insult, this intrusion.
Her fingers have grown used to the rise and roll
of a tiny pebble under the skin. She is playing
with her unmaking. The doctor offers
to remove it all, to take away the weight
of her old pleasures, to flatten the ground
she walks on, and only then, cupping
these ordinary things, does she begin to weep,
her body warming with the confusing
and overwhelming wash she cannot quiet.
This is a song of loss and the passing of light.

FISHING

Sunlight,
leaking from a slash wound
of yellow streams
of brightness
"Nana" – Ishion Hutchinson

1
Chasm

The day's heat still clings despite the growing gloom
of twilight. The lake stretches dumbly here in the gut
of the state. They push off – the ritual is calming –
their orange lifejackets, the ballasting of the child
in blankets to cradle him when the undulating
water rocks him softly, and she, sitting at the helm
peering out, her back to him. He has tried to read
its stoic guardedness, but the language is glutted
by resentments. On the drive down they talked of bills,
the schedule ahead, words arriving without prompting,
as if trying to empty themselves of ordinary chafes,
before the wide silence of the water.
Now, on the lake, she hums psalms. He has learned
the science of baiting in the dark. His line hisses
then grows silent. He waits for the tug, the feel
of life beneath them. She is a shadow across the divide.
It is easier to smell her – the fresh sweat, the faint perfume –
than to feel her. The child sleeps between them like a bridge.
To catch bass, one must pray softly, remain still,
allow the dark to lull you before the pull. Tonight,
nothing bites. He is rehearsing his tears and speeches
now, the fear that beneath this placid, familiar surface
is a void so complete, so irrevocably grand in its silences,
it could drown them. He dozes off from the heat
and the metronome of the lapping water,

then, dreaming, he awakes to find her gone – the boy
on a pillow floating among the reeds and rushes,
the moon growing over him. Though fleeting,
he regrets the relief he feels. He wakes again
when she says, "Let's go home. It's late."

2

Getting There

After John Sargent's "Paul Helleu Sketching with his Wife"

He rows alone, planting smoothed worn wood
softly into the current. He is mesmerized
by the sound of water parting, the whisper it makes
against the weathered flanks of the boat.
She stares into the sky, holding close to her chest
the damp paddle; it soaks into the fabric,
then into her skin. Her pout is gone.
She is cold already; fight no longer sustains her.
He grunts, "We are fighting the order of things;
you keep losing the rhythm; we will
go in circles if you don't let me do it."
How can she say to this logic:
"I dreamt we were doing it together,
I saw us moving with something
delicious – the pull and tug of lovers.
I imagined us cutting the surface like this
or at least trying and laughing about it."?
So he does, and at last the romance:
a lazy summer dusk, the moon growing
over the swamp's edge, the water
near tepid, a sullen amiable sluggishness,
the straw hats, the red ribbons,
the sports jacket, the wide skirt,
the satchel of paints and brushes,
the accoutrements of a picnic,
the orderliness of a boat drifting
across a placid lake, the pewter
and sepia rocks to the side. Then she says,
"No, you do it. I will watch."
He will ask her if she is happy,
if she enjoys the water, the view;

if she found his landscape, the humid
watercolour of a stunted dogwood
lovely and to her liking. She hears,
"Did you come?" and she answers,
as always with faith, "It was lovely,
you were lovely" – for that is enough.
She is holding the paddle to her breasts,
the hard handle pressing a nipple;
it will leave a mark on her skin.

3
Catch

There is in the sudden elation of a catch
a belief in miracles, as wide as hope.
For a moment there's dark,
a placid dense quiet in the gap between
lovers islanded on a boat drifting
over a lake, forty miles away from light,
from the miniature city where his mother
has prepared bowls of seasoned flour,
diced onions, peppers and garlic,
a cleared counter and a deep pot of oil
ready on the stove, as she watches
reruns of soaps, waiting for her son to return
with a fresh catch, her faith always firm,
a kind of conjuring that bemuses
all other distractions. This is what he
thinks about here on the lake – a mockery
of this silence between lovers, before
the exquisite chaos of a bite, then
the grunt and cheers of hauling it in.
The gift arrives with laughter and tears.
Who could imagine such elation in this
gleaming tangible thing? He hands it to her.
She can be forgiven for seeing him as a man,
a strong provider, hunter and progenitor;
he forgiven for the softening of pride he feels –
the dampness in his eyes. In that instant
he imagines the breaking of ties, the un-cleaving
from a mother's elastic umbilicus reaching
across the miles. She says, "Let's put it back."
And he says, "We are keeping this."
And she says, "We have eaten, already."
And he says, "For mother, she is waiting."

4
Nocturnal

There in the quiet of midnight, the body cleansed
of the detritus of gutted fish – only the iron smell
of blood still lingering in the nose – the house
is still rocking like a boat. He is snoring; everything
ticks with creaturely disquiet. She thinks
of the anatomy of orgasms, how they change each
time, how narrow they have become in closing walls
of pleasure. These days it is something fierce,
like resentful pain, a moment with no elasticity.
The after-effect is a dull high after the first
giddy years of surprise. Now, afterwards, she is able
to contemplate the menu for tomorrow, the errands,
chores, the cat litter she must buy, the eggs, the milk;
the poem she must write. Those long, stomach unfurling
transports are gone, the days when all she could wonder
was when the nervous pulsing would stop,
when the distended bloat and sweet pain
would subside, when her breath would return
and her skin would not jump at the breath of a breeze,
the suggestion of touch. Now her body aches
with the labour; she shouts harshly, almost a bark.
Now he doesn't care who hears; she says, maybe,
at least they will envy me, which is better than not.
Now she grinds out her desire like a short flame –
fast, then done. Dreams, though, multiply these days;
they come even while she is awake; they come
with the rush of clouds. She collects art, pictures
of women, hundreds of them. She stares long enough
at their complex of colours, then enters worlds
so far from her ordinary days. She floats through these
distractions with gladness, something like the way
she swims, head underwater, eyes closed tight,
arms moving furiously, the air pressed against her chest.

The sound is deep green and she pushes forward
hoping for the assurance of the bank. But as she
moves ahead, she is suspended in this postcard
painting of a fish cutting through tendrils and reeds,
light whipping past, remembering the world of that old,
glorious orgasm that used to unfold and unfold
for hours and hours and hours.

5

Mariana
After John Everett Millais' "Mariana"

There is a fresh Christian sincerity in hooking bass,
then unhooking the dumb mouths, feeling the muscle
of desperation in her hand. Then, after pictures,
she plants them in the lake, holding on long enough
to feel the sensuality of water warm in this June season –
the living pulsation before letting go – the bass falling
into ritual, another lesson of grace lost on it.
Her hands make things, embroidery of gothic elaboration –
a cloth stretched over her prayer table strewn with leaves
that have spilled through the stained-glass window
which overlooks her garden. At dusk, after the shower,
after the ordering of the household, she stands,
arms akimbo before the window, looking out as if she expects
someone to be looking back, and she averts her gaze
casually, waiting for the last light to flame her skin
into a mellow brownness, a colour so full of beauty
that it startled her once as she walked past a store window.
She wears her navy-blue coat, the one that clings
to her torso; the waist where her hands rest is smaller,
and she thrusts her chest forward, the white frills
framing the soft gutter of her bosom. She gives this
to the window, to the garden, to the light. She is fishing
for a compliment. Her reflection against the speckled window
seduces. But it is growing dark, now. A grey bass
is plunging deeply into the hollow of the lake. There is
hunger in her body's quiet desire that offers no language.
She smells the living death of fish in her fingers.
The prayer cloth is unfinished so she works, the crochet
needles moving in quick swirls like the breaking of the lake
before the boat's bow. At dawn, she will cover her head,
whisper a prayer while soft light catches her in dark garments,
like a girl returning from a clandestine party,
ready to repent of all her terrible sins.

6

Addiction

She has grown to love the rituals of fishing. Addiction
is too dramatic an analogy, but she is drawn to the open lake
in this dense heat of summer like she is drawn to those vices
that always left her hungry, tender and wondering what
the next time would be like. She sits in the kitchen
and the impulse crawls up her legs, like a voice whispering
its way into her damp places. She allows air in, a reflex
to cool the slow burn. It never stops until she stands,
walks to the window, stares into the sky, looking east
to their old town, as if she can see across the swamp,
the untidy pine forest, the trailer parks, then the long
wood-thick road that falls open at the muddy landing.
She calculates the clouds' weight, testing their messy
smudges of pewter, charcoal, indigo and grey,
to see how long she can stay dry there on the open water,
her lure settled low, her mind caught in the suspended place
between air and the dark mystery of the lake's belly.
The fear is still there. She trembles at the nudge of drifting
vegetation against the boat's skin, trembles as if it is
her body being invaded. But she can speak to the mute
watery shadows beneath the surface, and there on the water,
where all things move with the sluggish labour of a gorged hawk
rising into the sky, her pulse slows to a drugged slumber.
The nearer she comes to the water, the more
she understands myth: how a girl could talk to fish, kiss fish,
embrace the slimy fulsomeness of a speckled bass; how she,
a squeamish child, can enter this soft muggy world of earth smells,
blood, and the ammonia-scent of dead fish; how she can find
comfort in this place with its sweet release of addiction, before,
leaving it all behind, she drives away on the rain-slick road.

VESTAL
For my daughters

There are maps stained onto the surface
of these adobe walls – pulpy as ancient leaves
with the mess of history. Those long narrow
cracks on the surface are rivers travelling down
to the deltas where they branch off like roots
or cilia, or where, as with all ancient mysteries,
they trail off and vanish. Men piss against
the wall, the warmth turning the residue
into thick green algae, the rot of our colonial history.
This is the backdrop. The child, who leans
against the comfort of the uneven wall,
who relishes the cool caught inside the stone,
is one of those stray black children sprinting
through the lanes, sandalled and holy
as the vestal bride before her many wounds.
Ask her, if you dare, why she wears
her startlingly white embroidered scarf,
not to affect a nun's purity, but as something fluid,
a mocking masquerade. Ask her and she will say:
"It is my hair, it flows like a river, and when I flip it,
it bounces, see?" We are always grieving over
what we could not teach our dark-skinned daughters:
that they are beautiful for the deep brown
in them, for the onyx depth of their eyes,
for the fruit of their hips, for the assured substance
of their hair. The child dances in a quick twirl,
the scarf dancing through the air, then she
sprints down the street, laughing, laughing!

FEBRUARY LIGHT

For Lorna

The sky offers a brief mellow smile,
a calm pewter assurance, the gentle backdrop
against which the annual death of the sycamore
suggests a priest's instrument of blessing –
the aromatic twigs bundled and dipped in oil
to spray the gathered congregants, or a couple
distracted by the fear of a new beginning,
their awkward bodies learning to consider
coupling. This wash of morning sunlight
will pass quickly enough for us to remark
at the light of our days: "Can you see that?"
"Yes, it is beautiful." This is it: communion
in the grace of the earth's occasional beauty.

IN THIS SAYING

i

There is a way to end books –
the gathered papers, their weighty
gift, the clean parade of words

in columns of paragraphs and sequences
of images – the tidiness of things.
Numbered, they form the thing

you have laboured over for years.
To end a book, you tie a blue ribbon
around the heft, make a bow, kiss it.

ii

The way to end a year of cataclysms
is to find a piece of land by water,
where old boats rot at the edges,

and the place smells of ancient things –
sulphur, salt, rotting fish, and
the deep musk of mud and grass.

And then sit on a moving jetty,
rocking against the universe's
pulse, and there wait for the moon.

iii

To end this way alone, is to end
with the hollow melancholy
of loss and regret. Better to end

with the voice of your woman,
for you will need that voice,
ordinary as rain, speaking your name.

Perhaps it is the intrusion of her scent
filling the air, or the cool of her touch
fragrant with tomato pulp and herbs.

iv

Do not worry;
I know the genre
of this poem because

I know the name
of the bodies standing
in the dusk by water:

Kwame and Lorna.
They will hold hands,
and, in this saying, the poem ends.

STURGE TOWN REDUX

By three o'clock, the walls are stained with shadows,
these colonial walls that we have kept, despite the revolution
and the new dialect of independence, kept for their history.
Here, below the jutting balcony of wrought iron,
centuries of paint and rust create an artist's strip
of contained beauty, every blotch of paint, every spot
of decomposed dye like the artful peeling of brittle scabs –
first the quick pain, the pulsing, the soft seep of blood,
and then the pixilated skin. Below the makeshift clothesline,
a pair of loose-waisted red panties scar the deep purple
of a cave into the cheap rental it has been.
That simple moment, that piece of garment, that suggestion
of daily lives, ordinary, necessary, and mortal,
becomes the subject of this instant, the caught second
where the scene freezes and waits for the evaluation
of what we carry inside us.
                    What I must confess
is that the house, set on the face of a mountain,
surrounded by thick trees, despite the rot and decay,
has kept its shape, is the place I call an ancestral home,
though no one is sure where the deeds are,
and I have no head for real estate and inheritances,
just words to carve the fading permanence of memory.
Still, as if to plant a claim on the pimento barbecue,
there are the red panties, a kind of flag of ownership,
with not a soul in sight. I imagine a woman,
her skin deep as roasted coffee beans, lifting her gleaming
legs over the high grass and stones, peering around
to be sure she is not watched, clutching her bag
to her side, before she walks along the narrow road
down the hill. My cousin, perhaps, or a squatter
who has bartered for the birthright of my cousin
and my tribe. I will follow her on the road,
catch up to her, and then ask her, as casually as you offer

a stranger a glass of cool water, "Which part is home?"
And she will say, "Home is which part you want to bury",
as if that is the end of it, as if she can now turn a bend
in the road, step behind a roadside croton hedge
and vanish down a path into the dark valley.

ACKNOWLEDGMENTS

I would like to express my grateful acknowledgment to the editors of the following publications where earlier versions of these poems first appeared:

Adroit Journal: "Wanderer" and "Cathedral"; *BIM*: "The Reunion"; *Blackbird*: "Bones in the Soil"; *Crazyhorse*: "At the Cemetery"; *Grit Po: Rough South Poetry Anthology*: "Reburial"; *Indiana Review*: "Three Latter Day Duppies"; *Kenyon Review*: "Gated", "Making a Deal," "The Remnant," and "In this Saying"; *Locked Horn Literary Journal*: "After the Deluge"; *Narrative Magazine*: "Rehearsal for Lovemaking", and "The Forgettable Life"; *Obsidian II:* "Return"; *Oxford American*: "Work"; *Passages North*: "A Year"; *Plume*: "Washing Women"; *Poetry*: "Horns"; *Poetry Foundation*: "Vagrants and Loiterers" and "Ode to the Clothesline"; *Poets.org*: "It Bruises, Too" and "How I Pray in the Plague"; *Raleigh Review*: "Rain"; *Rattle*: "Sorrow"; *Spillway*: "Mourning Sky"; *Southeast Review*: "The Darkest Elation"; *The American Poetry Review*: "On Becoming," and "The Unspeakable Things"; *The Sewanee Review:* "Gardenia Leaf on a White Wall"; *The Southern Review*: "When Light Leaves Her Eyes"; *Southern Indiana Review*: "Light Home"; *The Georgia Review*: "Mendacity"; *The New Yorker*: "Eshu or Ambition"; *Transition*: "The Vanishing"; *Virginia Quarterly Review*: "Baptism of Dust", "Elegy for the Candle Maker", "When We Pray", "Faith Healing", "The Body"; *Washington Square Review*: "Mist"; *Yale Review*: "After the Biopsy" and "On Hearing the News of Another Shot Black Man".

ABOUT THE AUTHOR

Kwame Dawes is the author of over thirty books, and is widely recognised as one of the Caribbean's leading authors. He is Glenna Luschei Editor of *Prairie Schooner* and a Chancellor's Professor of English at the University of Nebraska. His previous book from Peepal Tree Press was *unHistory*, with John Kinsella, the fifth book of poems written in this partnership. He was born in Ghana, grew up in Jamaica and has lived most of his adult life in the USA.